Macroeconomics:

Principles and Their Applications

Macroeconomics: Principles and Their Applications

Author: KANG Jae Taeck
Publisher: HAN Heon Joo
Ppublishing company: Kyung Mun Sa
Address: 21-9, Dongnimmun-ro, Seodaemun-gu, Seoul, Korea
Phone: 02) 738-7035
FAX. 722-4678
E-mail : kmsp@korea.com
http://www.kmsp.co.kr
First printing is 2018. 09. 05

Price 20,000 Won

ISBN 978-89-420-0893-3 93320

Author Page

- **Name** : KANG Jae Taeck
- **Education** :
  - 1982. Graduated from Yonsei University, Seoul (BA, Economics)
  - 1991~1993. Doctoral coursework, Paris XIII University (DEA, International Economics)
  - 1997~2000. Ph.D (Paris XIII University), National Diplome
- **Career** :
  - The Bank of Korea, the nation's central bank (1982~present)
- **Books** :
  - The Recent Debate on the New International Financial Architecture (2003.1. The Bank of Korea)
  - The Exchange Rate in Our Daily Life (2008.4. Kyung Mun Sa)
  - 21st Century Currency Wars: The Challenge of the Yuan and the Future of the dollar (2014.12. Maekyung Daily)
- **Teaching** :
  - Principles of Macroeconomics: Underwood International College, Yonsei University (2015~)
  - Exchange Rate and Foreign Exchange Market: the Bank of Korea (2016~)
  - Exchange Rate, International Finance: Korea Banking Institute (2007~2012), Korea Institute of Financial Investment (2008~2012)

Preface

This book is different from the existing books in the following ways:

First, this book explains the main contents of macroeconomics based on 14 topics. During one semester we have 14 weeks of lectures, in addition to the two weeks for the midterm and final tests. The readers will come to understand one topic every week.

Some topics are however divided into two parts, for example Monetary Economics I and Monetary Economics II.

Second, this book explains each topic starting from the basic concept and moving all the way to the high level theory, including the limitations on applying the theory in the actual economy. The readers will thus come to understand each topic systematically, learning the basic concept first, followed by the details, limitations and applications of the topic.

Third, this book focuses on the development of reasoning. Macroeconomics explains our daily life in the diverse areas of the macro economy. The students of this class should thus be able to explain the recent global and domestic macroeconomic situations, together with offering some proposals for relevant policy measures.

This part is the relatively strong point of this book, which I can illustrate based on my career at the Bank of Korea from 1982 up until now.

In writing this book, I was helped by many persons. Mr. Michael Marking edited my poor English. Mr. KIM Tae Saup and Mr. YUN Se Jin provided support with some of the graphics and data.

I hope that this book will be useful to readers in learning the principles of macroeconomics.

September. 2018.

KANG Jae Taeck

Contents

(Week 1)

Measuring a Nation's Income: GDP

1. Concept

- **Economic data provide a systematic and objective source of information.**
  - 3 major macro data: There are 3 major macro data indicators – GDP, the CPI, and the unemployment rate.

- **GDP (Gross Domestic Product): GDP is the market value of all final goods and services produced within a country during a given period of time.**
  - Market value
    - The term "market" means the legal market. Thus, any goods and services traded in an illegal market or in an underground market are excluded in the GDP.
    - Market value means a value measurable by a market price. Thus, some services such as housekeeping or cooking home meals are left out of the GDP, because their values are not measurable by market prices.

■ Final goods

- Only final goods are included in the GDP. Thus, no intermediate goods used in the production of final goods are counted as parts of the GDP.
- For example, if a certain amount of sugar is purchased to put into a cup of coffee, then this sugar is consumed as a final good and is included in the GDP.

  But sugar used at a bakery to make bread is not consumed as a final good, but used as an intermediate good to make the bread. It is thus not included in the GDP, and only the bread is.

■ Services

- Services are intangible products that are not manufactured. Services become more and more important in the GDP as the economy develops.

■ Within a country

- Any product made within a country is included in its GDP. Thus, even if a product is made by a foreigner residing in that country, it is included in the GDP.

- Given period of time
  - GDP is measured quarterly as well as yearly. Quarterly data are sometimes converted to annual basis data, and this process is called annualization.

– GDP: Equality of income and expenditure

- The total income of everyone in the economy should equal the total expenditure on the economy's output of goods and services. This is because every transaction has a buyer and a seller, and the buyer's expenditure should equal the seller's income.

2. Components of the GDP

– GDP is composed of four factors:

$$Y = C(Y-T) + I(Y, i) + G + NX(X-M)$$

- Consumption: $C(Y-T)$

- Consumption means goods and services bought by households. Here, goods include nondurable goods such as clothes, vegetables, etc. and durable goods include for example cars, machinery, etc.
- Used goods are excluded from the GDP. This is because used goods were already included in the GDP in the past when they were produced.
- Imputed rents on owner-occupied homes are included in the consumption. These imputed rents are estimated as consumptions expenditure by renters using the available data on rental prices of similar homes.

  If they didn't own their homes, the owners would have to pay rents, and their consumption expenditures should therefore be less than at present, by the estimated amounts of these rents.
- $C(Y-T)$ means that consumption depends on the disposable income after taxes. When disposable income increases so does consumption, but the amount depends on how much of the increased disposable income is consumed, that is the so-called marginal propensity to consume (MPC).

■ Investment: $I(Y, i)$

- Investment means goods bought for future use, and these goods create a new physical asset, capital. Investment includes three categories:

  ① business fixed investment, which means purchases of new plants and equipment,

  ② residential fixed investment, which means purchases of new housing, and

  ③ inventory investment, which means the increase in goods that firms have produced but not yet sold. Because these goods are unconsumed and kept for future use, they are considered as investment.

- Inventory investment should be monitored carefully when evaluating the GDP growth rate. If an economy's high growth rate is due mainly to an increase in inventory, it does not mean a good performance of the economy. An increase in inventory means that consumption was less than expected, and that the total demand of the economy was lower than its output. In this economy, output should then decrease until the inventory disappears.

  When looking at the GDP growth data, therefore,

careful interpretation is needed in order to understand the actual economic situation correctly.

- Household purchases of new housing: Purchases of new housing by households are considered as investments. This is because people buy houses to get housing services in the future.
- $I(Y, i)$ means that the investment decisions depend on output and on the interest rate.
  ① When output increases, sales also increase while inventory decreases. Firms need to expand their investments to increase their production. There is thus a positive relationship between investment and output.
  ② When the interest rate rises, the cost of borrowing to buy new machines increases and investment falls. There is thus a negative relationship between investment and output.

■ Government Expenditure (G) and Taxes (T)

- G means government spending, and describes fiscal policy implementation together with taxes T. But G and T have different multiplier effects.

① Effect of ΔG: If the government expands expenditures by ΔG, then this causes consumption to increase by the same amount as ΔG. This increase in consumption causes consecutive increases in consumption to infinity, depending on the marginal propensity to consume (MPC). The total effect of increasing demand in the economy is as follows:

$$\Delta G + \Delta G \cdot \text{MPC} + \Delta G \cdot \text{MPC}^2 + + + + +$$
$$= \Delta G (1 + \text{MPC} + \text{MPC}^2 + + + + +)$$
$$= \Delta G \cdot \{1/(1 - \text{MPC})\}$$

② Effect of ΔT: If the government decreases taxes by ΔT, this causes people's disposable income to increase by ΔT. This increased disposable income leads to a rise in consumption affected by the MPC starting from $\Delta T \cdot$ MPC, and this rise in consumption causes consecutive increases in consumption to infinity, depending on the marginal propensity to consume (MPC). The total effect of increasing demand in the economy is as follows:

$$\Delta T \cdot \text{MPC} + \Delta G \cdot \text{MPC}^2 + \Delta G \cdot \text{MPC}^3 + + + + +$$
$$= \Delta T (\text{MPC} + \text{MPC}^2 + \text{MPC}^3 + + + + +)$$

$= \Delta T \cdot \{\text{MPC}/(1-\text{MPC})\}$

- If the government increases spending by ΔG with a simultaneous increase in taxes by $\Delta T (\Delta G = \Delta T)$, then we have two kinds of increases in output:

  ① The increases in output due to the different multipliers, which are as follows:

  $\Delta G \cdot \{1/(1-\text{MPC})\} - \Delta T \cdot \{\text{MPC}/(1-\text{MPC})\}$,

  with $\Delta G = \Delta T$

  $= \Delta G \cdot [\{1/(1-\text{MPC})\} - \{\text{MPC}/(1-\text{MPC})\}]$

  $= \Delta G \cdot \{(1-\text{MPC})/(1-\text{MPC})\}$

  $= \Delta G$

  Because the multiplier of ΔG is larger than that of ΔT, the economy has a net increase in consumption of ΔG.

  ② The increases in output due to different MPCs.

  An increase in taxes is focused largely on the wealthy class, whose MPC is relatively lower than that of the poor class who should be the beneficiaries of the increase in government expenditure.

Thus, the decline in consumption resulting from a tax increase should be less than the rise in consumption due to an increase in government expenditures. The total demand of the economy and output should both increase.

- When the government increases spending by ΔG through issuing government bonds, we have to consider two factors that offset the multiplier effects of ΔG:

① The crowding-out effect

In an economy, the total capacity to buy bonds is limited and the total demand for bonds is limited as well. This is called limited credit availability.

Under this limited credit availability, if the government increases the supply of bonds then the remaining market capacity to buy other bonds, for example corporate bonds, decreases. This pushes up the corporate bond and market interest rates.

A rising interest rate discourages investment and causes output to decline. This is called the "crowding-out effect," because the increased government bonds crowd out the demand for private sector bonds.

② The appreciation effect

A rising interest rate in an open economy

When a country's interest rate rises, the return on investment in this country's assets rises as well. If all other things remain unchanged, the demand for this country's currency in order to buy this country's assets increases. The currency of this country should appreciate, making its price competitiveness weaker. Exports should decrease and imports increase. Thus net exports (exports minus imports) decrease and output decreases as well.

- When the government reduces taxes by ΔT to promote consumption, we have to consider one offsetting factor of the multiplier effect, the so-called "Ricardian Equivalence."

After a tax cut, disposable income increases transitorily but people cannot consume all of this increased income. They expect that the government will raise taxes in the future, since it cannot sustain a budget deficit forever. People therefore save some part of their transitorily increased incomes to prepare for a possible future tax increase. This saving offsets the effect of the tax cut.

How much of this increased income should be saved is dependent on people's expectations of the future increase in taxes. If people save the entire amount of their increased income for the expected future tax increase, their savings completely offset the increase in their disposable incomes. This idea was raised by Ricardo, and is referred to as Ricardian Equivalence.

- Net Exports: $NX(X-M)$
  - Net exports (NX) are the difference between exports (X) and imports (M), and thus $NX=X-M$.
  - Exports (X) mean the goods and services produced within a country but purchased by foreigners. Because these goods and services are not purchased by domestic residents they are not included in C, I or G. But because they are produced within the country they should be included in its GDP. And so they are classified as exports (X), a part of GDP.

- Imports are goods and services not produced within a country but purchased by its domestic residents. They are included in GDP as C or I or G, but should not be. We thus have to subtract imports from GDP.
- If exports exceed imports, then the net exports are positive and the current account shows a surplus. If exports are less than imports, then the net exports are negative and the current account is in deficit.

3. Nominal GDP and Real GDP

– Nominal GDP

■ Nominal GDP is the sum of the quantities of final goods and services produced times their current prices. Nominal GDP thus increases over time with the increases in the production of goods and in the prices of goods.

Table 1. Nominal GDP volumes of major countries

(billion dollars)

	2013	2014	2015	2016	2017
United States	16,692	17,428	18,121	18,624	19,391
Euro area	13,195	13,498	11,668	11,940	12,607
China	9,635	10,535	11,226	11,222	12,015
Japan	5,156	4,850	4,395	4,949	4,872
Germany	3,754	3,897	3,377	3,479	3,685
United Kingdom	2,742	3,024	2,886	2,661	2,625
France	2,809	2,854	2,435	2,466	2,584
Korea	1,306	1,411	1,383	1,411	1,538
Norway	524	499	387	371	396
Luxembourg	62	66	58	59	62

Source: IMF

Gross domestic products

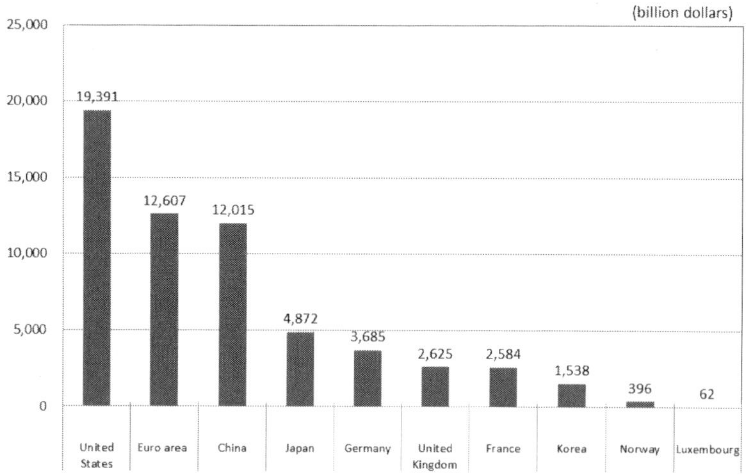

Note: 1) As of 2017

Source: IMF

■ Nominal GDP shows the size or the structure of the economy.

- **Real GDP: at constant prices, growth rate**

■ Real GDP is the sum of the quantities of final goods and services produced, times their constant prices. Here constant prices mean the prices of goods of the base year.

• Real GDP therefore increases over time with the increases in the production of goods only, and not with the increases in the goods' prices.

■ Real GDP is used to analyze the growth or fluctuations of the economy.

• The growth rate of the economy is calculated as follows:

$$\text{Growth rate of period } t \ (\%) = \frac{\text{real GDP}_t - \text{real GDP}_{t-i}}{\text{real GDP}_{t-i}} \times 100$$

For yearly growth rate: $i=1$
For quarterly growth rate: $i=1$ or $i=4$

If $i=1$, we have the quarterly growth rate against the preceding quarter. Here we have to convert this three-month period of economic growth to growth on a one-year basis through multiplying it by 4, a process called annualization.

If $i=4$, we have a quarterly growth rate against the same quarter of the preceding year.

– GDP deflator

■ The GDP deflator in year t is defined as the ratio of the nominal GDP to real GDP in year t, as follows:

$$\text{GDP deflator} = \frac{\text{Nominal GDP}_t}{\text{real GDP}_t}$$

• Even if real GDP does not change, a change in prices can cause nominal GDP to increase. Thus, in order to check whether an increase in nominal GDP comes from a rise in prices or from an increase in the quantity of the production, we have to divide the nominal GDP by the real GDP. If this ratio is larger than 1, the increase is due to the effect of prices.

■ GDP deflator and inflation:

• The GDP deflator shows the general price level of the total product of a country. Thus a rise in the

GDP deflator compared to the preceding year means inflation of the total product.

$$\text{Inflation } (\pi\ t,\ \%) = \frac{\text{GDP deflator}_t - \text{GDP deflator}_{t-1}}{\text{GDP deflator}_{t-1}} \times 100$$

– Potential GDP

- Potential GDP means the GDP that a country can produce with a full employment level of labor and with a normal level of operation of capital.
  - Potential GDP is a long-term concept, and equivalent to output at full employment or to the natural rate of output.

- GDP gap: The GDP gap is the difference between the actual GDP and the potential GDP.

  GDP gap = Actual GDP – Potential GDP

  - If the GDP gap is positive, this means that the production factors are being used to a more than normal extent, and that the economy is in a boom. A positive GDP gap shows the inflation pressures on the demand side.
  - If the GDP gap is negative, it means that the pro-

duction factors are being used less than they are in a normal situation, and that the economy is in a contraction.

– Purchasing Power Parity GDP

■ Every country has a different level of GDP and a different price level. If country A's per capita GDP is 50,000 dollars and country B's is 10,000 dollars, then we can evaluate that country A's people have 5 times more purchasing power than country B's people.

- This evaluation is correct if country A's price level is exactly equal to that of country B. But if country A's prices level is twice as high as country B's, then the purchasing power of the people in country A is just 2.5 times that of those in country B. This is because country B's purchasing power parity GDP is double that of country A.

Table 2. Per capita GDPs of major countries

(dollars)

	2013	2014	2015	2016	2017
Luxembourg	115,006	120,853	102,688	101,797	105,803
Norway	102,722	96,838	74,281	70,652	74,941
United States	52,737	54,657	56,411	57,559	59,501
Germany	46,545	48,119	41,345	42,250	44,550
France	44,105	44,572	37,866	38,205	39,869
United Kingdom	42,767	46,820	44,328	40,530	39,735
Japan	40,490	38,156	34,612	38,983	38,440
Korea	25,890	27,811	27,105	27,535	29,891
China	7,081	7,702	8,167	8,116	8,643

Source: IMF

Per capita gross domestic products

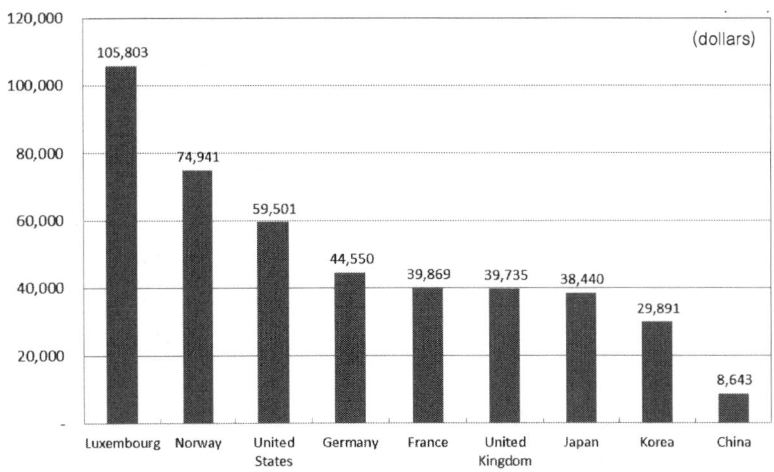

Note: 1) As of 2017

Source: IMF

Table 3. Purchasing power parity GDPs of major countries

(billion dollars)

	2013	2014	2015	2016	2017
China	16,689	18,229	19,698	21,290	23,159
United States	16,692	17,428	18,121	18,624	19,391
Japan	4,899	5,006	5,129	5,243	5,429
Germany	3,639	3,776	3,874	3,997	4,171
United Kingdom	2,510	2,633	2,724	2,812	2,914
France	2,542	2,612	2,669	2,735	2,836
Korea	1,699	1,787	1,857	1,934	2,029
Norway	335	347	358	367	380
Luxembourg	51	55	57	60	63

Source: IMF

Purchasing power parity GDPs

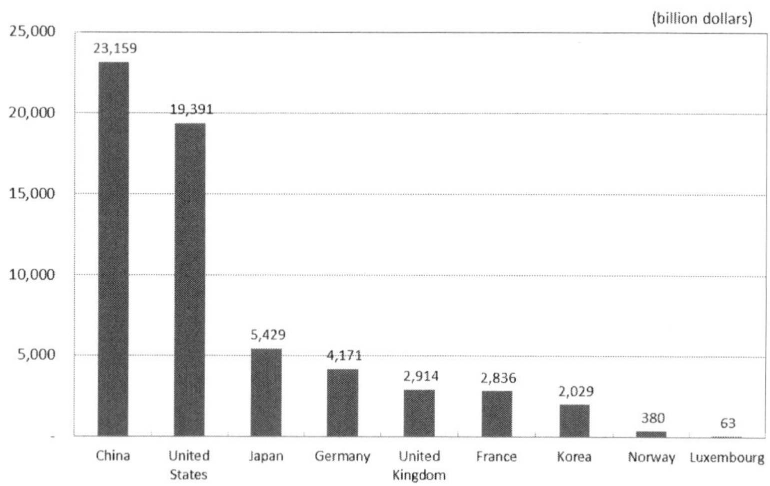

Note: 1) As of 2017

Source: IMF

4. Limitations of GDP

- **GDP is relatively the best indicator of the people's standard of living, but it still has some limitations.**

■ Limitations

- GDP does not show the quality of life reflecting social welfare, the social infrastructure and the price level.
- The aforementioned factors actually affect the real disposable incomes of the people.

■ No alternative

- Even though it has some limitations, there is in reality no alternative that can replace GDP. Economists therefore discuss ways of overcoming the limitations of GDP and of ameliorating the GDP data.

5. GDP and Market Variables

- **GDP is the most important macroeconomic data. When the GDP data is announced, market variables react to this.**
- **We have to analyze the impacts on market variables due to the GDP announcement in three steps: positive data, news, RO–RO (risk on-risk off). Here we analyze the US GDP data announcement and the case of the US dollar as an example.**

■ First step: Positive data

- We may think that good US GDP data will cause the dollar to appreciate. If the US GDP data is good then the value of US assets is expected to rise. Thus, the demand for US assets should increase and the demand for the dollar should increase as well.
- But this reasoning is not always accurate. Why? Because market variables do not respond to the present data itself but to the expectations that the data implies. In other words, market variables respond to the news.

- Second step: News
  - Market variables respond to the news. This is because the existing public information is already reflected in the market variables.
  - If the US GDP data is good, and better than expectations, then market participants become optimistic about the US economy and will want to buy US assets. The US dollar should appreciate due to the increased demand for US assets.
  - If the US GDP data is good but below expectations, then market participants become pessimistic about the US economy and will want to sell US assets. The dollar should depreciate due to the decreased demand for US assets.

- Third step: Risk-On and Risk-Off (RO-RO)
  - After the global financial crisis of 2008, market participants showed a new phenomenon – the so-called Risk-On and Risk-Off behavior.
  - If the US GDP data is better than expected, and already at the same time the GDP data of other major countries are also better than expectations,

market participants can anticipate a recovery of the global economy. They can purchase relatively risky assets, expecting relatively higher returns. The demand for safe currencies, especially the dollar, decreases and the demand for risky currencies grows. The dollar can depreciate even with better GDP data than had been expected. This is the so-called Risk-On behavior.

- If the US GDP data is worse than expected, and already at the same time the GDP data of other major countries are also worse than expectations, the market participants are still skeptical about the recovery of the global economy. They can purchase relatively safe assets and safe currencies like the dollar. The demand for the dollar can thus increase, causing dollar appreciation even with worse GDP than had been expected. This is the so-called Risk-Off behavior.

■ The Great Rotation

- The terms Risk-On and Risk-Off are now frequently used as market jargon.
- When market participants respond first to the global market risk rather than to the economic data of indi-

vidual countries, we can easily see these Risk-On and Risk-Off behaviors. Such a change in the attitudes of market participants, from focusing on the economic data of individual countries to global risk, is called in the market a Great Rotation, and the reverse change is called a Reverse Great Rotation.

(Week 2)

Measuring the Cost of Living: CPI

1. Concept

– CPI: Consumer Price Index

- The CPI shows the average price of a specific list of goods and services having different weights.

- Like the GDP deflator the CPI is an index, and is set equal to 100 in the base year.

– Core CPI

- The Core CPI means the CPI excluding the volatile food and energy prices.

- For example, if oil prices double due to a rise in geopolitical risk, or if food prices rise rapidly due to extraordinary cold or hot temperatures, the CPI rises steeply to reach a level higher than the CPI target of the central bank.

- If the central bank implemented its monetary policy by focusing only on the CPI, which is volatile as seen in the aforementioned cases, then the central bank would have to tighten monetary policy in a very strict way, causing a severe contraction of the economy.

CPI and Core CPI trends

■ Korea

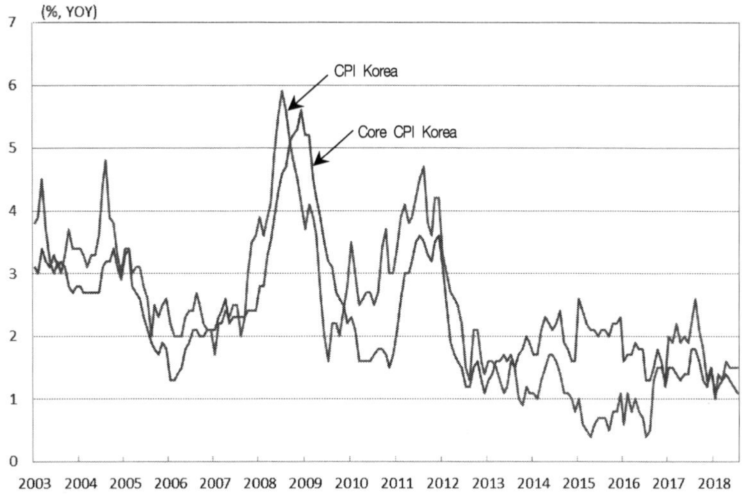

■ US

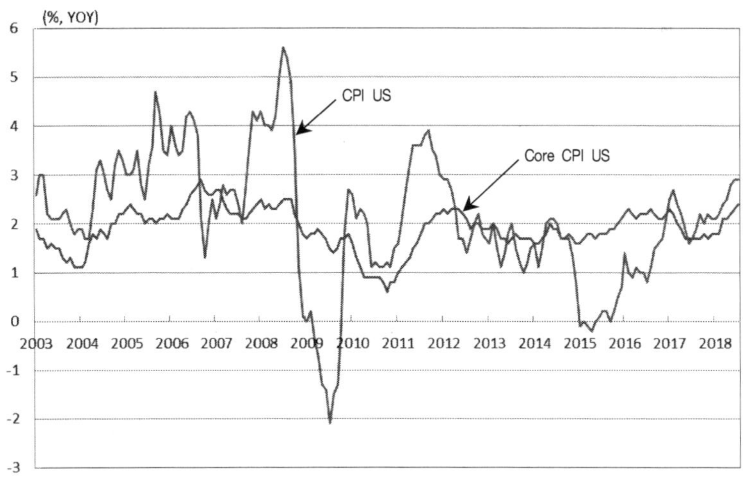

- If the central bank implemented its monetary policy with a focus not only on the CPI but also on the Core CPI, then it could more carefully and more flexibly evaluate the movements of prices reflecting the fundamental trends of the economy. The central bank could avoid causing any unnecessary fluctuations of the economy.

2. Calculating the CPI

- **Calculating the CPI involves two steps:**
  - First, fixing the basket of the important goods and services with different weights is necessary.
  - Second, after choosing the base year, and giving its CPI the value of 100, the other years' CPIs.
- **Inflation Rate**
  - Inflation means the change in the CPI compared to

the preceding year. The inflation rate is thus calculated as follows:

$$\text{Inflation } (\pi\ t,\ \%) = \frac{CPI_t - CPI_{t-1}}{CPI_{t-1}} \times 100$$

where CPI_{t-i}: CPI of the preceding year, year t-1,
CPI_t: CPI of the present year, year t

3. PPI

– PPI: Producer Price Index

- The PPI measures the cost of a basket of goods and services bought by firms to produce some goods.

- Firms buy goods in order to produce consumption goods. If the prices of these goods bought by the firms rise, then the costs of production rise. The firms should raise the prices of their consumption goods in order to maintain their mark-ups and profits.

- Thus, if the PPI rises then the CPI should follow and

CPI and PPI trends

■ Korea

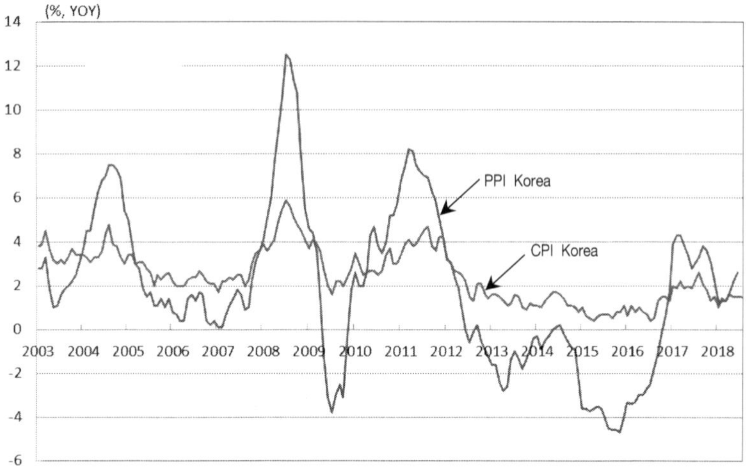

■ US

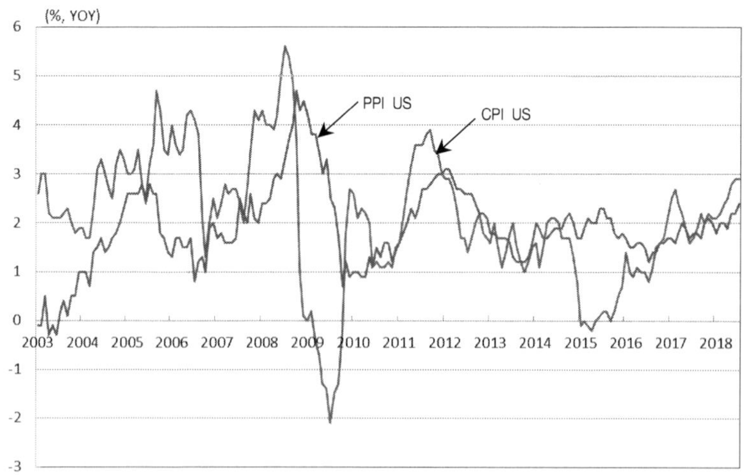

rise as well. The PPI therefore shows the future direction of the CPI, and is a leading indicator of the CPI.

4. The CPI and the GDP deflator

– **Both the CPI and the GDP deflator show the movements of the prices of consumption goods and services. But there are some differences between them, as follow:**

■ Capital Goods

- When the prices of the capital goods produced within a country rise, the GDP deflator also rises because these capital goods are included in the GDP.
- But the CPI does not change, because these capital goods are not included in the consumption goods.

- Imported Goods
  - When the prices of the imported goods which are consumed within a country rise, the GDP deflator does not change because these imported goods are not produced in the country and are not included in the GDP.
  - The CPI does change, however, because these goods are consumed in the country.
- Flexibility of goods weights
  - The CPI is calculated with a fixed weight given to each good and service included in the CPI basket.
  - The GDP deflator is calculated by dividing the nominal GDP by the real GDP, without considering the weight of each good and service. In the GDP deflator, therefore, the weights of the goods and services are flexibly and automatically changed by the values of nominal GDP and real GDP.

5. Real Interest Rate and Nominal Interest Rate

– **Inflation causes the real value of the nominal interest rate to fall. Thus, in order to secure the real value of the nominal interest rate after inflation, the nominal interest rate should increase.**

- If we have an $i\%$ nominal interest rate per year on a bank deposit, and the inflation rate for the year is $\pi\%$, then the real interest rate is $(i-\pi)\%$. This relationship comes about as follows:

  $$\frac{(1+i)}{(1+\pi)}=(1+r), \text{ thus } (1+i)=(1+r)\cdot(1+\pi)$$

  $$1+i=1+r+\pi+r\pi,\ i\doteqdot r+\pi,\ i=r+\pi$$

  Cancelling 1 on both sides and neglecting $r\pi$, which is very small, we have the aforementioned relationship.

– **Ex post real interest rate and ex ante real interest rate**

- We have the relationship $i=r+\pi$, and so $r=i-\pi$.

- Ex post real interest rate: When we analyze the economic situation using the past inflation data, we use the existing real interest rate data by $r = i - \pi$. In this case the real interest rate is the ex post rate, which shows the past economic situation.
- Ex ante real interest rate: When we make an investment plan for the future, we have the data of the nominal interest rate i, but don't have the data on present inflation π due to the time lag in statistics. In this case we have to use the expected value of inflation π^e, and the real interest rate becomes $r = i - \pi^e$. This is called the ex ante real interest rate.

When the central bank determines its monetary policy plan, it should use the expected value of inflation π^e to fix the target interest rate. The target real interest rate is therefore an ex ante concept.

6. Indexation

- **Indexation is the automatic correction made in accordance with law or with the terms of a business contract, to protect the value of the nominal interest rate from the effects of inflation.**

  ■ The US Treasury Department issues securities that are protected from inflation, the so-called TIPS (Treasury Inflation Protected Securities).

  - The TIPS pay returns as follows: principal $\cdot (1+\pi) \cdot (1+i)$
  - The amount of TIPS principal is automatically changed based on the inflation rate $(1+\pi)$, and the nominal interest rate $(1+i)$ is thus secured for the investor irrespective of the inflation rate.
  - Because these TIPS are protected from inflation, their interest rates are relatively lower than those of normal Treasury securities without inflation protection.

7. Deflation

- **Deflation: Deflation means a decrease in the price level from the preceding year, so that the inflation rate is negative.**

  ■ In a deflation situation, people delay their buying of goods and services in anticipation of being able to purchase them more cheaply later. Inventories therefore increase, causing declines in investment, total demand and output.

- **Deflation and the Monetary Policies of Central Banks**

  ■ Abenomics: In order to escape deflation, Japanese Prime Minister Abe announced in 2012 a plan to increase the quantity of Japanese Yen issuance without limit until the CPI reaches 2%. This is called Abenomics.

    • Abenomics and the debate over currency manipulation: After the announcement of Abenomics, there was some debate about whether this policy of increasing the issuance of the Japanese Yen was a kind of currency manipulation or not.

Argument of currency manipulation: Some countries argued that an increase in the supply of an international currency should clearly cause it to weaken, and that this depreciation of the currency should be seen as intentional. Thus, the weakness of the Japanese Yen was a de facto kind of currency manipulation.

Japan's policy defense: Japan insisted that it never intervened in the foreign exchange market by selling yen and buying dollars to cause the yen to depreciate. Japan argued that the weakness of the yen since the start of Abenomics was just a by-product of the increase in the monetary supply to escape deflation.

Support from USA: The US defended Japan in the international community, based on the following reasoning: that Japan wasn't intervening in the foreign exchange market, and the recovery of the Japanese economy should be beneficial to the world economy as a whole. After recovering, Japan would increase its imports of goods from other countries.

- NIRP (Negative Interest Rate Policy): Some central banks have adopted negative interest rate policies to break out of recessions.
  - NIRPs were introduced based on expectations that they should discourage people from depositing money and encourage them to consume more instead.
  - If people had to pay some of their money as the cost for depositing it in a bank account, rather than receiving interest on it, then they should minimize their deposits if possible. But other alternatives to bank deposits are limited. Keeping cash at home is not only dangerous, but also costly in that home security systems are not free.
  - Therefore, the maximum negative interest rate that people can accept is the level of the cost arising from keeping their cash at home.

Table 4 Central banks with negative interest rates

Country	Introduced	Present
Eurozon	June 2014, deposit rate cut to –0.1%	–0.4%, since March 2016
Bank of Japan	2016 at –0.1%	Still in effect
Swedish Riksbank	Feb 2015, repo rate cut to –0.1%	Repo rate at –0.5%, since February 2016
Swiss National Bank	January 2014 at –0.25%	–0.75%, since January 2015
Denmarks Nationalbank	July 2012, main policy rate at –0.2%	–0.75%, since early 2015

Source: Negative Interest Rates, S&P Global, August 17, 2016

8. Disinflation

- **Disinflation: Disinflation means a decline in inflation while it is still positive. The policy of a central bank to lower the economy's inflation rate to a reasonable level is disinflation.**
  - When inflation is higher than the inflation target, the central bank should implement monetary tightening, i.e. a raising of the target interest rate.

- Here, the central bank estimates how much the target interest rate should be raised, by applying a "Monetary Policy Rule" or the so-called "Taylor Rule" as follows:

$$ff_{target} = \pi + r_n + 1/2(\pi - \pi_{target}) + 1/2(\text{GDP Gap, \%})$$

$$ff_{target} - \pi = r_n + 1/2(\pi - \pi_{target}) + 1/2(\text{GDP Gap, \%})$$

where r_n: natural rate of real interest,
ff_{target}: federal funds target rate,
GDP Gap (%): GDP growth rate - Potential GDP growth rate

  - Implication: This rule implies that if the inflation rate (π) rises above its target (π_{target}) by 1%p, then the real federal funds target rate ($ff_{target} - \pi$) should be raised by 0.5%p (we will discuss this rule in detail in Week 9).

(Week 3)

The Unemployment Rate and the Phillips Curve

1. Breakdown of the Adult Population

- **Members of the adult population are classified as in the labor force (*L*) or not in the labor force (*NL*).**

  - The labor force is composed of the employed (*E*) and the unemployed (*U*).

    - The employed (*E*) are adults who have intentions to find jobs and actually have jobs.
    - The unemployed (*U*) are adults who have intentions to find jobs but do not actually have jobs.

  - The category "not in the labor force" refers to adults who are out of the labor force because they are not looking for jobs. Such a person is therefore neither employed nor unemployed, as for example a student.

2. Unemployment Rate (u)

- **The unemployment rate is one of the three major macroeconomic indicators referred to by central banks including the US Federal Reserve.**
- **The unemployment rate (u) is calculated as follows:**

$$u = \frac{\text{Number of unemployed } (U)}{\text{Labor force } (L = E + U)} \times 100\ (\%)$$

- **Meaning of the unemployment rate**
  - In general, when the unemployment rate rises higher than the central bank's target or than its long-run equilibrium level, the economy becomes less dynamic than the central bank wishes. The central bank's monetary policy will in this case tend to be more accommodative.
- **Limitations of the unemployment rate, and the LMCI (Labor Market Conditions Index)**
  - In some cases, the unemployment rate may not be able to completely show the actual labor market situation.

- Giving up on looking for jobs: If people give up on looking for jobs, they are by definition out of the labor force. Thus the number of the labor force (L) and that of the unemployed (U) decrease together, leading finally to a decline in the unemployment rate even through there is in reality no change in the actual labor market situation.
- Incompletely employed: Employed people include those who do not work sufficient hours to pay their living expenses. As one example, in Korea a person who works more then 1 hour during the census week is included among the employed. But this person cannot earn enough salary to live based on 1 hour of work per week. We can thus say that he or she is not completely employed.

■ LMCI (Labor Market Conditions Index): The US Fed and many other central banks use the LMCI as an auxiliary indicator of the labor market, to make up for the limitations of the unemployment rate. This LMCI shows various conditions of the labor market.

3. Identifying Unemployment

- **Natural rate of unemployment and cyclical unemployment**

  ■ The natural rate of unemployment is the normal rate of unemployment, also known as the non-accelerating inflation rate of unemployment (NAIRU).

  ■ Cyclical unemployment is a deviation of unemployment from its natural level.

- **Job search and frictional unemployment**

  ■ Frictional unemployment occurs due to mismatches between the demand for and the supply of labor. Such mismatches can be of the following types:

  • Mismatches between worker's preferences and abilities and the job's characteristics

  • Mismatches in information about job candidates and job vacancies due to imperfect flows of information

  ■ Frictional unemployment can also occur due to a sectoral shift.

- If a new industrial sector develops, then the demand for labor in this industry increases but the demand for labor in other sectors decreases.

■ Policies to reduce frictional unemployment

- Dissemination of information: Government agencies disseminate information about job vacancies in order to match jobs and workers. Such a policy can minimize the mismatches in information about job candidates and job vacancies, and help to reduce frictional unemployment.
- Retention programs: Publicly funded retention programs are offered to ease workers' transitions from one sector to other sectors. They can help workers to more easily adapt to new jobs, and frictional unem- ployment should decrease.

■ Unemployment insurance: The government pays an unemployed person a certain percentage (e.g. 50%) of her former wage for some period. Unemployment insurance has positive effects and negative effects.

- Positive effect: An unemployed person can take the time needed to find a high quality job thanks to receiving unemployment insurance, and can thus achieve a higher standard of living.

- Negative effect: The better the unemployment insurance, the less active the unemployed become in searching for work. The unemployment period thus lasts longer, and the related moral hazard increases.

– **Structural unemployment due to wage rigidity**

■ Minimum wage laws: Minimum wage laws set a legal minimum wage that firms must pay their employees, which is higher than the equilibrium wage.

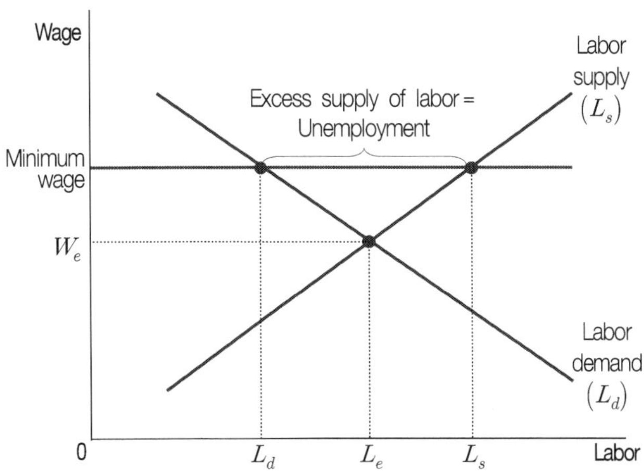

- Positive effects: A minimum wage law raises the incomes and living standards of the working poor. Their increase in income leads to increased consumption, which boosts the total output of the economy.
- Negative effects: First, an increase in wages due to a minimum wage law results in greater inflation pressures. Second, a minimum wage law heightens the wage burdens of firms, which may lead them to reduce their employment hours or numbers of persons employed to maintain their total labor costs. Third, if the increase in wages due to a minimum wage law is higher than the increase in the productivity of a firm, the competitiveness of the firm declines.

■ Labor unions: A labor union can keep wages above the equilibrium level through collective bargaining or labor strikes.

- Positive effects: First, labor unions can secure sufficient wages and good working conditions for member employees. Second, a labor union can protect member workers from unfair work demands and unfair layoffs from their jobs.

- Negative effects: First, due to the higher wages demanded by labor unions firms employ less than the equilibrium number of employees, and unemployment increases. Second, if the increase in wages negotiated by a labor union is higher than the increase in the productivity of a firm, the competitiveness of that firm weakens.

■ Efficiency wage: The efficiency wage theory says that higher wages make workers more productive.

- Positive effects: An efficiency wage can lead to increased productivity due to improved nutrition and health, and to lower turnover and higher loyalty of workers. Firms can increase their productivity by hiring workers of better quality and higher loyalty.
- Negative effects: If the enhancement of its productivity is lower than the increase in its wages, then the competitiveness of a firm declines. If a competitor that pays relatively lower wages produces a competing product, then the firm cannot survive due to its weaker price competitiveness.

4. Unemployment and the Phillips Curve

– Original Phillips Curve

- In 1958, A. W. Phillips discovered a negative relationship between inflation and unemployment.
  - The data that he used were the annual rates of inflation and unemployment in the United Kingdom from 1861 to 1957.

- In 1960, Paul Samuelson and Robert Solow also found a negative relationship between inflation and unemployment in the United States, and named this relationship "The Phillips Curve" (Original Phillips Curve).
  - They used the data on CPI inflation from 1900 to 1960.
  - They found that when unemployment was low, inflation was high, and when unemployment was high inflation was low:

$$\Pi_t = (m+z) - a \cdot u_t$$

where Π_t: inflation,
m: mark-up,

z: catch-all variable,
u_t: unemployment rate,
a: parameter that captures the effects of unemployment on wages

– Modified Phillips Curve

■ In the 1970s most OECD countries experienced both high inflation and high unemployment, which contradicted the Original Phillips Curve theory.

- A new relationship was found between the changes in inflation and the unemployment rate.
- In the United States, a high unemployment rate leads not to low inflation but to a decrease in inflation.
- Conversely, a low unemployment rate does not lead to high inflation but to an increase in inflation.

$$(\Pi_t - \Pi_{t-1}) = (m+z) - a \cdot u_t$$

– General form of Phillips Curve

■ Generalizing the two aforementioned cases, we have the following equation:

$$\Pi_t = \theta \cdot \Pi_{t-1} + (m+z) - a \cdot u_t$$

- If θ is 0, $\Pi_t = (m+z) - a \cdot u_t$ (Original Phillips Curve)
- If θ is 1, $(\Pi_t - \Pi_{t-1}) = (m+z) - a \cdot u_t$ (Modified Phillips Curve)

■ But because the inflation expectation (Π_t^e) is dependent on past inflation (Π_{t-1}), $\Pi_t^e = \theta \cdot \Pi_{t-1}$ and the generalized Phillips Curve $\Pi_t = \theta \cdot \Pi_{t-1} + (m+z) - a \cdot u_t$ becomes $\Pi_t = \Pi_t^e + (m+z) - a \cdot u_t$ and $(\Pi_t - \Pi_t^e) = (m+z) - a \cdot u_t$.

■ When unemployment is at its natural rate, $u = u_n$, $P = P^e$, and $\Pi_t = \Pi_t^e$, and so $(\Pi_t - \Pi_t^e) = 0 = (m+z) - a \cdot (u_t = u_n)$, and $(m+z) = a \cdot u_n$.

$(\Pi_t - \Pi_{t-1}) = (m+z) - a \cdot u_t$ becomes $(\Pi_t - \Pi_{t-1}) = a \cdot u_n - a \cdot u_t$, and $(\Pi_{t-}\Pi_{t-1}) = a(u_n - u_t)$, $(\Pi_t - \Pi_{t-1}) = -a(u_t - u_n)$.

- We thus have a negative relationship between disinflation $(\Pi_t - \Pi_{t-1})$ and the deviation of the unemployment rate from its natural level $(u_t - u_n)$.

  When the unemployment rate is higher than its natural level $(u_t > u_n)$ the inflation rate decreases $\{-(\Pi_t - \Pi_{t-1})\}$, and when it is lower than its natural level $(u_t < u_n)$ the inflation rate rises $\{+(\Pi_t - \Pi_{t-1})\}$.

– Disinflation and the Sacrifice Ratio

- If we want the inflation rate to fall, then we need to accept a rising unemployment rate through the following relationship:

$$(\Pi_t - \Pi_{t-1}) = -a(u_t - u_n)$$

  - If a is estimated at 0.55, then $u_t > u_n$ by 1% means 0.55% disinflation $(\Pi_t - \Pi_{t-1})$. For 1% disinflation, therefore, we need (1/0.55) = 1.8% of $(u_t > u_n)$.

– Okun's Law

- Okun showed the negative relationship between unemployment and growth.

  - If the growth rate rises, then the unemployment rate falls:

$$u = a - 0.4 \text{ growth rate (example)}$$

- If we combine the Phillips Curve and Okun's Law,

$$(\Pi_t - \Pi_{t-1}) = -0.55(u_t - u_n), \quad u = a - 0.4Y$$

  - For 1%p disinflation, we need a 1.8%p higher unemployment rate, and this means a (1.8/0.4) = 4.5%p sacrifice of the growth rate.

(Week 4)

Production and Growth

1. Solow Model

– Concept

- The Solow growth model shows how growth in the capital stock (K), growth in the labor force (L) and advances in technology (TP, technological progress) interact in an economy, and how they affect a nation's output.
  - In the Solow model capital (K) is defined as physical capital, the set of tools that workers use such as cranes, calculators, PCs, etc.
  - Labor (L) is defined as the time that people spend working.
  - Technological progress is assumed to come from outside the economic system. The Solow model is thus called an exogenous growth model.

– Production Function

- The Solow growth model assumes that the production function has a constant return to scale:

$$Y = F(K, L)$$

$$zY = F(zK, zL) \leftarrow \text{constant return to scale}$$

$$Y/L = F(K/L, 1), \leftarrow z = 1/L$$

$$y = f(k),$$

where K: physical capital,
L: labor,
$y = Y/L$ as output per worker,
$k = K/L$ as capital per worker

- Diminishing Marginal Product of Capital (MPK↓): The slope of the production function declines. This means that the extra output due to the input of an extra unit of capital, that is the marginal product of capital (MPK), decreases:

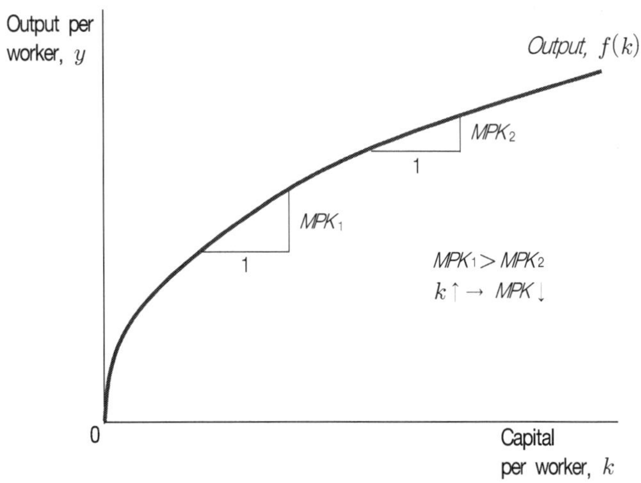

- MPK= $f(k+1)-f(k)$ decreases: If k increases then y increases, but y increases less and less as k becomes larger and larger.

■ Technological progress (TP) can shift the production function $y=f(k)$ upward. But technological progress is not explained in the Solow growth model, and is considered to come from outside the economic system. This model is thus called an exogenous growth model.

– The demand for goods and the consumption function

■ The demand for goods in the Solow growth model comes from consumption and investment:

$$y=c+i$$

where y: output per worker (Y/L),
c: consumption per worker (C/L),
i: investment per worker (I/L)

- Here, if s = the savings rate, then the amount of savings per worker $s \cdot y$ equals the output per worker (y) – the consumption per worker (c). Thus, $s \cdot y = y-c$, and $c=y(1-s)$.

- Using the aforementioned relationship,

$$y = c + i = y(1 - s) + i,$$

$$y = y - y \cdot s + i,$$

$$i = s \cdot y$$

We get the relationship $i = s \cdot y$, which says that the investment per worker equals the savings per worker (this is called the national income identity).

- Growth in capital stock and the steady state

- Investment in new plants and equipment causes the capital stock to increase:

$$i = s \cdot y = s \cdot f(k)$$

- But old capital wears out gradually and the capital stock decreases due to depreciation:

$$\text{depreciation} = \delta k$$

where δ: depreciation rate

- The change in the capital stock equals investment – depreciation:

$$\Delta k = i - \delta k = s \cdot f(k) - \delta k$$

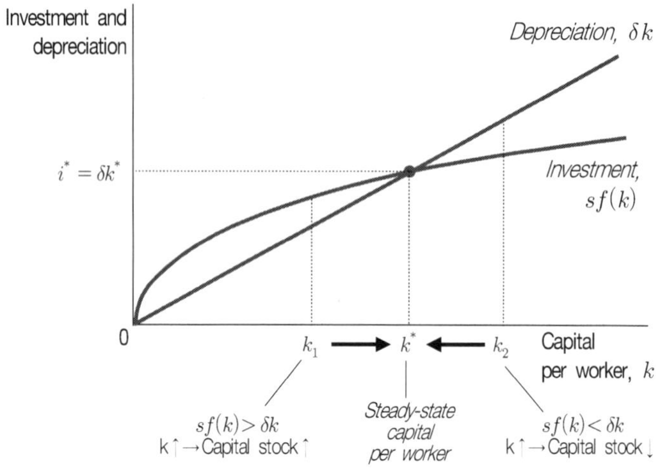

If $s \cdot f(k) = \delta k$, i.e. if investment (=savings) equals depreciation, then $\Delta k = 0$. The capital stock and output are steady over time at the k^* level, and k^* is thus called the steady-state level of capital.

– Effect of savings on growth

- When the savings rate increases ($s_1 \rightarrow s_2$) but the capital stock and depreciation remain unchanged, the capital stock rises to a new higher steady-state level:

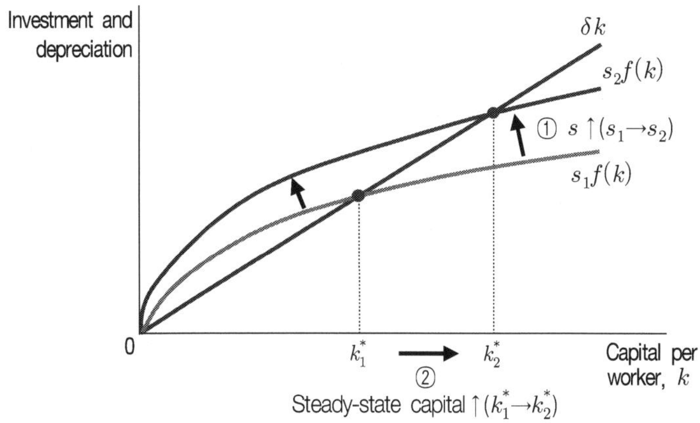

- Higher savings ($s_1 \rightarrow s_2$) leads to faster growth in the Solow model, but only temporarily from the k_1^* steady-state level to the k_2^* steady-state level.

– The Golden Rule

■ The Golden Rule level of capital is the steady-state value of capital k that maximizes consumption:

$$
\begin{aligned}
c^* &= y^* - i^* \\
&= f(k^*) - i^* \\
&= f(k^*) - \delta k^* \leftarrow \text{in the steady-state,} \\
&\qquad\qquad \Delta k = 0,\ i^* = \delta k^*
\end{aligned}
$$

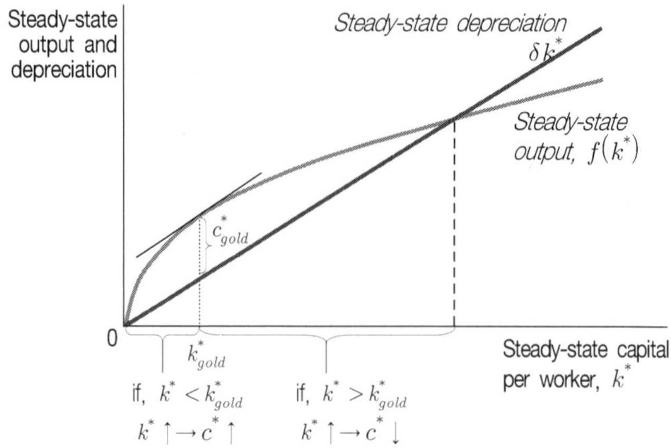

- c^* reaches its maximum where the slope of $f(k^*)$, MPK, equals the slope of δk^*, δ. Thus, at the Golden Rule k^*, k^*_{gold}, MPK= δ.

– Population Growth

- If the population and the labor force grow at the rate n, then in order to keep the capital per worker (k) constant, more investment is needed.

- If the capital depreciates at the rate δ, then in order to keep the capital per worker (k) constant, more investment is needed:

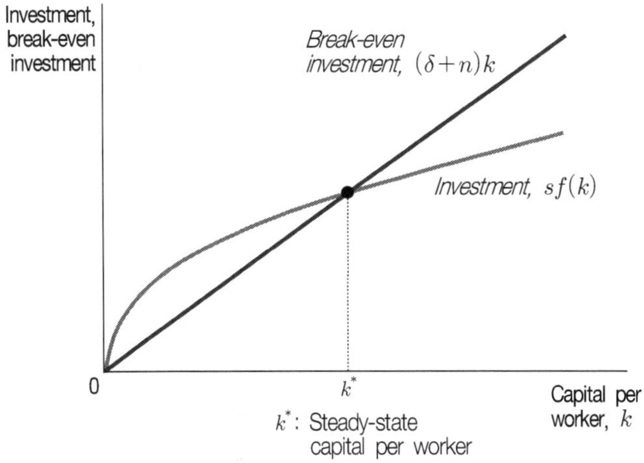

■ Thus, the break-even level of investment becomes $(\delta+n)k$:

$$\Delta k = s \cdot f(k) - (\delta+n) \cdot k$$

■ In the Solow model, countries with higher rates of population growth (n) will have lower levels of capital and income per worker in the long run.

- Golden Rule with Population Growth

■ We express c^* in terms of the capital stock to find the Golden Rule:

$$c^* = y^* - i^*$$

$$= f(k^*) - i^*$$

$$= f(k^*) - (\delta + n)k^*$$

- c^* reaches its maximum where the slope of $f(k^*)$, MPK, equals the slope of $(\delta+n)k^*$, $\delta+n$. Thus, at the Golden Rule k^*, k^*_{gold}, MPK$=\delta+n$.

– Technological progress in the Solow model

■ Labor augmenting technological progress causes the efficiency of labor to increase at the exogenous rate g.

$$Y = F(K, LE),$$

where E: labor efficiency,
EL: effective worker

$$zY = F(zK, zLE), \leftarrow \text{ constant return to scale}$$

$$Y/LE = F(K/LE, 1), \leftarrow z = 1/LE$$

$$y = f(k), \ g = \Delta E/E$$

■ Increases in labor efficiency have the same effect on output as increases in the labor force.

- If the labor efficiency increases at the rate g, then more investment is needed to keep the level of capital per effective worker constant:

$$\Delta k = s \cdot f(k) - (\delta + n + g) \cdot k$$

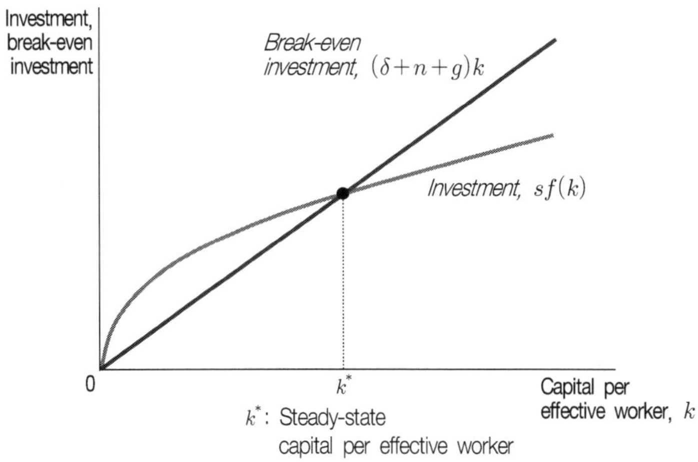

- Golden Rule with technological progress

- We express c^* in terms of the capital stock to find the Golden Rule:

$$
\begin{aligned}
c^* &= y^* - i^* \\
&= f(k^*) - i^* \\
&= f(k^*) - (\delta + n + g)k^*
\end{aligned}
$$

- c^* is at its maximum when the slope of $f(k^*)$, MPK, equals the slope of $(\delta+n+g)k^*$, $\delta+n+g$. Thus, at the Golden Rule k^*, k^*_{gold}, MPK$=\delta+n+g$.

– Implications of the Solow model

- In the steady state, the rate of growth in output per worker depends on g, the rate of increase in labor efficiency. Thus, only technological progress can lead to sustained growth in output per worker.

  - In the steady state, the level of capital per effective worker ($k = K/LE$) is by definition steady.

    Thus $\Delta k = 0$ and $\Delta k/k = \dot{k} = 0$.

  - In the steady state, the level of output per effective worker ($y = Y/LE$) is by definition steady.

    Thus $\Delta(Y/LE) = 0$ and $(Y/\dot{L}E) = 0$.

  - In the steady state, the level of output per worker, ($y = Y/L$), equals $(Y/LE) \cdot E$.

    Thus, $\Delta\{(Y/LE) \cdot E\} = \Delta(Y/LE) + \Delta E$,

    $$\{(Y/L\dot{E}) \cdot E\} = (Y/\dot{L}E) + \dot{E} = 0 + g$$

  - In the steady state, total output, Y, equals $\{(Y/L) \cdot LE\}$.

    Thus, $\Delta\{(Y/LE) \cdot LE\} = \Delta(Y/LE) + \Delta(LE)$

    $$\{(Y/L\dot{E}) \cdot LE\} = (Y/\dot{L}E) + (\dot{L}E) = 0 + n + g$$

- A high rate of savings leads to a high rate of growth until the steady state is reached. But beyond that there is an over-accumulation of capital that sacrifices consumption and causes dynamic inefficiency.

- Convergence issue: Each economy approaches its own steady state.
  - Convergence: If two countries have different starting points in terms of capital per worker and the same inherent steady-state levels, then they will converge to the same steady-state level.
  - No convergence: If two countries have different starting points in terms of capital per worker and different steady-state levels, then they will reach different steady-state levels. There is thus no convergence.
  - Conditional convergence: If two countries are in similar economic situations, then they have similar starting points in terms of capital per worker and similar steady-state levels. They can thus converge, depending on economic performance.

- Factor accumulation and production efficiency: Nations with high levels of physical and human capital tend to use these factors efficiently. The interaction of physical and human capital is important.

- Limitation of Solow model: The Solow model shows that technological progress can lead to sustained growth in output per worker. But in this model technological progress is an assumed exogenous factor, with no explanation of its origin

2. Endogenous Growth Model

– Concept

- The endogenous growth model defines capital as including not only physical capital but knowledge as well. In this model a constant return to scale is thus more plausible.
  - The production function of the endogenous growth model is set as follows:

    $Y = AK,$

where K: capital including knowledge (and thus no diminishing return to scale, and A: total factor productivity.

$\Delta K = sY - \delta K$, investment−depreciation

$= sAK - \delta K$, ← $Y = AK$, dividing both sides by K

$\{\Delta K/K\} = \{sAK/K\} - \{\delta K/K\}$

$= sA - \delta$

$= \{\Delta Y/Y\} \leftarrow Y = AK$

– **Implication**

- If $sA - \delta > 0$, then $\{\Delta K/K\} > 0$ and the economy's income grows forever.
  - In the Solow model, savings leads temporarily to growth, but the diminishing returns to capital (MPK ↓) force the economy to approach a steady state, in which growth depends only on the exogenous TP.
  - In the endogenous growth model, however, savings and investment can lead to persistent growth due to the constant return to capital. This constant return to capital is possible if knowledge is viewed as a type of capital that has the property of non-rivalry and positive externalities.

2-1. Romer Model

Concept

- Romer showed the possibility of increasing returns due to the non-rivalry of ideas.
  - Output (Y_t) is produced using the stocks of knowledge (A_t) and labor (L_{yt}):

$$Y_t = A_t L_{yt} \cdots\cdots ①$$

with the following assumptions: 1) constant returns to objects (workers), 2) increasing returns to ideas (and objects) due to the non-rivalry of ideas, and 3) a distinction between ideas and objects

  - New ideas are produced using the existing ideas (A_t) and workers (L_{at}):

$$\Delta A_{t+1} = A_{t+1} - A_t = zA_t L_{at} \cdots\cdots ②$$

z: productivity parameter

  - Resource constraint: Total labor (L) is composed of labor for the object output (L_{yt}) + labor for the idea output (L_{at}):

$$L = L_{yt} = L_{at} \quad \cdots\cdots ③$$

- Allocation of labor in research and ideas (a), in output production ($1-a$):

$$L_{at} = aL,\ L_{yt} = (1-a)L \quad \cdots\cdots ④$$

- From ①, we get $Y_t = A_t L_{yt}$, and dividing both sides by L:

$$\frac{Y_t}{L} = \frac{A_t L_{yt}}{L} = \frac{A_t(1-a)L}{L} = A_t(1-a) \quad \cdots\cdots ⑤$$

- From ②, we have $\Delta A_{t+1} = zA_t L_{at} = zA_t aL$, ($\leftarrow$ from ④, $L_{at} = aL$), dividing both sides by A_t:

$$\frac{\Delta A_{t+1}}{A_t} = \frac{zA_t aL}{A_t} = zaL = g, \text{ a constant value} \quad \cdots\cdots ⑥$$

This means that the growth of knowledge ($\Delta A_{t+1}/A_t$) is constant over time ($zaL = g$) and proportional (z) to the number of researchers ($L_{at} = aL$).

- From ⑥, we have $\dfrac{\Delta A_{t+1}}{A_t} = \dfrac{zA_t aL}{A_t} = zaL = g$

$$\Delta A_{t+1} = A_t \cdot g$$

$$A_{t+1} - A_t = A_t \cdot g$$

$$A_{t+1} = A_t \cdot (1+g)$$

- By the following procedure,

$$A_{t+1} = A_t \cdot (1+g) = A_0 \cdot (1+g)^t \cdot (1+g) = A_0 \cdot (1+g)^{t+1}$$

$$\uparrow$$

$$A_t = A_{t+1} \cdot (1+g) = A_0 \cdot (1+g)^{t+1} \cdot (1+g) = A_0 \cdot (1+g)^t$$

$$\uparrow$$

$$A_{t-1} = A_{t-2} \cdot (1+g) = A_0 \cdot (1+g)^{t-2} \cdot (1+g) = A_0 \cdot (1+g)^{t-1}$$

$$\uparrow$$

$$\vdots$$

$$\uparrow$$

$$A_3 = A_2 \cdot (1+g) = A_0 \cdot (1+g)^2 \cdot (1+g) = A_0 \cdot (1+g)^3$$

$$\uparrow$$

$$A_2 = A_1 \cdot (1+g) = A_0 \cdot (1+g) \cdot (1+g) = A_0 \cdot (1+g)^2$$

$$\uparrow$$

$$A_1 = A_0 \cdot (1+g)$$

We thus have the relationship $A_t = A_0(1+g)^t$.

– Implications of the relationship $A_t = A_0(1+g)^t$

- The researchers create new ideas, whose rates of growth are unlimited.
  - These new ideas can provoke sustainable growth in income over time because they do not have diminishing returns thanks to the non-rivalry of ideas.

3. Productivity and Competitiveness

- **Productivity: The concept of productivity refers to how much the product can increase due to the addition of one unit of the production factor.**

  ■ Y/L: Labor productivity means how much the product can increase due to one additional unit of labor.

  ■ K/L: Capital productivity means how much the product can increase due to one additional unit of capital can increase.

  ■ Interaction: Labor and capital interact in production.

  - A smart human being can use a machine more efficiently, and cause the total factor productivity to increase.
  - With more advanced machines, the capacity of a smart labor force can be maximized.
  - We therefore have to consider capital as including not only physical capital but also human capital with non-rivalry. These two kinds of capital interact to lead total factor productivity to increase.

- Competitiveness

- Price Competitiveness: A product is competitive in price when it is sold at a lower price than those of other products of similar quality.

  - Price elasticity: If the price of one product among products of similar quality falls, then the demand for it increases. And if the price of this product rises, then the demand for it decreases. If the price elasticity is larger than 1, this product is price elastic.

$$\text{price elastic} = \frac{\Delta Q/Q}{\Delta P/P} > 1$$

  - Currency depreciation: In the export market, currency depreciation is an important factor determining price competitiveness. (see Week 11)

- Non-price Competitiveness: Other factors than its price can also affect the competitiveness of a product, and this is called non-price competitiveness.

  - If a product shows a very good, inimitable quality, then the demand for it is not much affected even with a rise in its price. Its price elasticity is thus less than 1, and this product is price inelastic.

- Determinants of non-price competitiveness: A good's quality is the most important determinant of its non-price competitiveness. However, there are other factors that also determine non-price competitiveness, such as customer service, sales networks, etc.

– Productivity and Competitiveness

■ An enhancement of productivity can lower the cost of production and raise the quality of a product.

- If the price of a good can become lower than before due to decreased production costs, then its price competitiveness improves.
- If the quality of a good is better than before due to an enhancement in productivity, then the price of this good can be raised without a decrease in sales.

■ An enhancement in productivity can thus ameliorate the competitiveness of a product in terms not only of its price competitiveness but also of its non-price competitiveness. In this case both the domestic and global market shares of this product can be increased.

(Week 5)

Savings, Investment and the Financial System

1. Financial System and Financial Market

- **Financial system: The "financial system" is the broad term for the institutions in the economy that facilitate the flows of funds between savers and investors.**
- **Financial markets: The financial markets are the places where savers provide resources for investment.**
  - Market for bonds: A bond represents a loan from the bond holder to the issuer, a firm. The buyer of a bond thus becomes a creditor of the firm, and the firm's issuing of bonds is debt financing.
  - Market for stocks: A share of stock represents a partial ownership claim by the shareholder in the issuing firm. The stock buyer thus becomes a part owner of the firm, and the firm's issuing of stocks is equity financing.
- **Financial intermediation: Financial intermediaries take funds from savers and provide them for in-**

vestment, and this function of theirs is called financial intermediation.

- Banks: Banks take deposits from savers and lend them to investors.
  - Banks pay lower interest rates to relatively short-term depositors, and receive higher interest rates from relatively long-term investors who borrow the deposited funds from them.
  - The difference between these deposit and lending interest rates is the main source of profit for banks, and is called the interest rate spread.

2. Some topics related to financial intermediation

- **Asymmetric information: Asymmetric information comes from the fact that the lender does not have all information about the borrower.**

- Asymmetric information concerning the financial situations of borrowers causes adverse selection.
  - Asymmetric information: The borrower wants to get the best conditions of borrowing, i.e. the lowest level of interest rate and the maximum amount of funds borrowed from banks. The borrower thus wants to show to banks a maximum amount of good information and a minimum amount of bad information.
  - Adverse selection: Financial intermediaries can decide to supply funds to borrowers that are not in the best financial situations because these borrowers are more active in trying to borrow funds from them. This is called adverse selection.
- Asymmetric information concerning borrowers' actions can bring about moral hazard.
  - Asymmetric information: Banks cannot know whether the borrowers will make optimal investments with the money that they have borrowed from them.
  - Moral hazard: Once a borrower has obtained funds from a bank, the borrower may pursue a maximum profit by investing in highly risky assets. If this

strategy succeeds then the borrower can enjoy a maximum profit after paying the already fixed interest rate. If this strategy fails, however, the borrower may announce a default with the loss attributed to the lending bank. This is called the moral hazard problem.

This moral hazard problem is more prominent when the borrowing firm operates a staff compensation system based on performance. In such a system, a higher return on investment secures a higher performance salary for the employee who made the investment.

This moral hazard risk of performance-based compensation systems can also be found in banks. If a bank manager receives a salary based on performance, then she may pursue high risk investments with the depositors' money. If such investments succeed the manager receives a higher performance salary. If they fail then the manager will just quit the bank and the loss will be attributed to the bank.

- **System risk, the lender of last resort, and moral hazard**

- System risk: If a significantly important bank goes into bankruptcy, it cannot make its payments owed to other banks. These other banks will then be unable to make their payments to other banks.

  In this case the entire banking system faces a failure of payments, and the banking system stops functioning. The risk of this happening is called system risk.

- The lender of last resort: In order to avoid system risk, central bank can supply funds to a bank facing such an inability to make its payments. This role of the central bank is called that of "the lender of last resort."

- Too big to fail and moral hazard: When a bank goes into bankruptcy, its size is an important factor causing system risk.
  - If a bank's assets under management are small, then its failure will be tolerable in the financial system. The central bank will not supply funds to this bank as the lender of last resort.
  - If a bank's assets under management are very large, however, then its failure will have sequential bad

impacts on other banks, and finally on the financial system as a whole. The central bank should supply funds to this bank, as the lender of last resort, in order to avoid a meltdown of the financial system.

- Here we have the so-called "too big to fail" issue. If a bank's assets are very large, then its failure will mean a melting down of the country's financial system. The central bank cannot let this bank go bankrupt, because it needs to maintain a functioning financial system. This is another case of possible moral hazard involving the bank's manager.

– Implementing the lender of last resort function

■ Distinguishing illiquidity from insolvency: Before helping a financially distressed financial institution, the central bank should evaluate whether that financial institution is facing illiquidity or insolvency.

- Illiquidity means a temporary lack of liquidity to pay debts for an institution with sufficient assets whose value exceeds that of its liquid debts.

- Insolvency means a lack of liquidity to pay debts for an institution with total asset of less value than its debts. Even the liquidation of all of its assets is thus not enough to repay its debts.

- Different interest rate policy for lender of last resort
    - Slightly higher interest rate for illiquidity: The central bank can help an illiquid financial institution so as to avoid system risk, by charging a slightly higher interest rate than in normal cases. The illiquidity problem is considered to be unintentional, and so a penalty interest rate is not needed. But in order to minimize moral hazard and to encourage prudential management, a slightly higher interest rate is recommendable.
    - Penalty interest rate for insolvency: The central bank can help an insolvent financial institution if doing so is unavoidable in order to prevent system risk. But the insolvency comes from the imprudent strategy of the financial institution, and the cost is borne by the people. The central bank should thus impose a high level of penalty rate, so as to minimize moral hazard.

      If the financial institution is not capable of accepting this high level penalty interest rate, then it should be nationalized after receiving the supply of central bank liquidity. Since the bank has been saved by the people's money, it should be put under the people's control.

- **Financial regulation**
  - Since a default by a systemically important bank causes system risk and requires support from the lender of last resort, the banking sector is regulated very strictly by the government and the central bank.

3. Market for Loanable Funds

- **Concept: The concept of the market for loanable funds is important for understanding the mechanism through which the interest rate is decided.**
- **Equilibrium in loanable funds market**
  - Supply of loanable funds: Savers supply loanable funds by buying bonds as demanders of bonds.
    - If the market interest rate rises, then the return from buying bonds, or the income from saving, rises, and

the supply of loanable funds increases. There is thus a positive relationship between the interest rate and the supply of loanable funds. The loanable funds supply curve shows an upward slope:

$$i \uparrow \rightarrow \begin{cases} \text{return on bonds} \uparrow \rightarrow \text{supply of loanable funds} \uparrow \\ \text{income on savings} \uparrow \text{(demand for bonds} = \text{Bd} \uparrow) \end{cases}$$

- Demand for loanable funds: Investors demand loanable funds by issuing bonds at the cost of the interest rate.
  - If the market interest rate rises, then the cost of borrowing, or the cost of issuing bonds, increases, and the demand for loanable funds falls. There is thus a negative relationship between the interest rate and the demand for loanable funds. The loanable funds demand curve shows a downward slope:

$$i \uparrow \rightarrow \begin{cases} \text{cost of bonds} \uparrow \rightarrow \text{demand for loanable funds} \downarrow \\ \text{cost of borrowing} \uparrow \text{(supply of bonds} = \text{Bs} \downarrow) \end{cases}$$

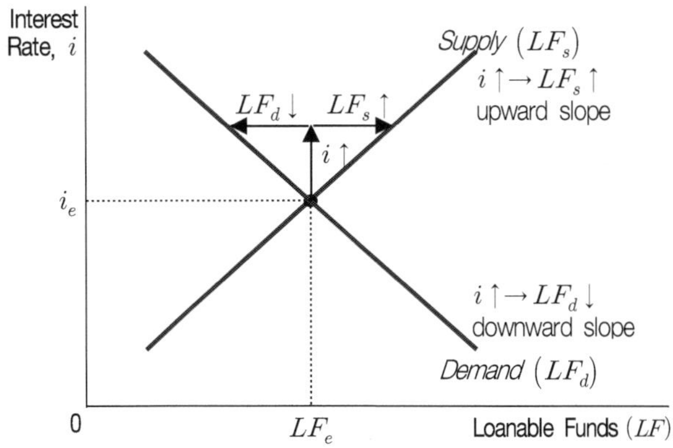

- **Tax incentives for saving**

■ Tax incentives for savings cause increased savings, i.e. the supply of loanable funds (LF_s) and the demand for bonds (B_d), for all levels of the interest rate. The loanable funds supply curve thus shifts to the right. $(LF_s \rightarrow LF_s')$

- As a result, the supply of loanable funds increases $(LF \rightarrow LF')$ and the interest rate decreases $(i \rightarrow i')$.
- We thus have the following relationship:

Tax incentives for loanable funds → Supply of loanable funds increases $(LF_s\uparrow)$ → Demand for bonds increases $(B_d\uparrow)$ → Price of bonds rises $(B_p\uparrow)$ → Interest rate falls $(i\downarrow)$

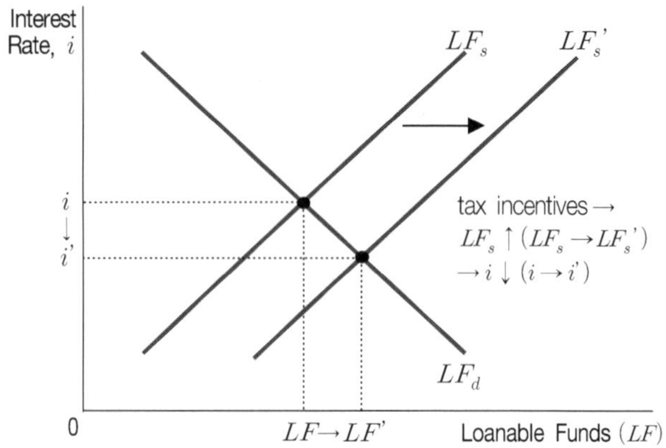

- Investment incentives

- Investment incentives lead to increased investment, i.e. the demand for loanable funds (LF_d) and the supply of bonds (B_s) increase for all levels of the interest rate. The loanable funds demand curve thus shifts to the right ($LF_d \rightarrow LF_d'$).

  - As a result, we have increased loanable funds demand ($LF \rightarrow LF'$) and a rise in the interest rate ($i \rightarrow i'$).
  - We thus have the following relationship:

    Investment incentive → Demand for loanable funds increases ($LF_d \uparrow$) → Supply of bonds increases ($B_s \uparrow$) → Price of bonds falls ($B_p \downarrow$) → Interest rate rises ($i \uparrow$)

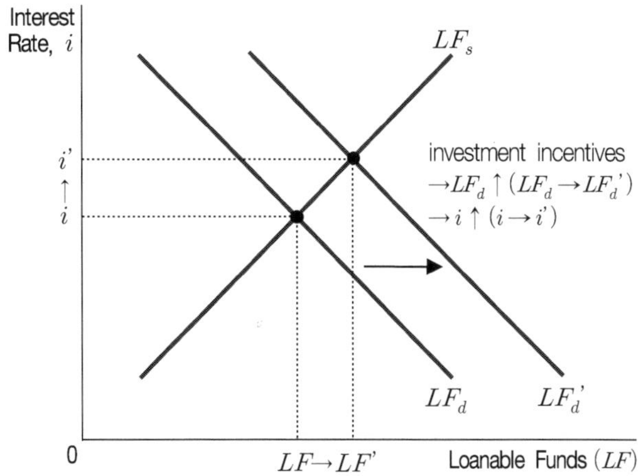

- **Government budget deficit**

■ The government budget deficit should be financed by issuing government bonds, which means an increase in the government bond supply.

- However, the maximum market capacity to buy bonds, or the maximum funds of the loanable funds market, is limited. This situation is called limited credit availability.
- Under this limited credit availability, the increase in the government bond supply crowds out the capacity to buy other bonds, e.g. corporate bonds.
- As a result we have a relatively decreased loanable

funds supply $(LF_s \rightarrow LF_s')$ compared to the increased demand for loanable funds, and an increased interest rate $(i \rightarrow i')$.

- We thus have the following relationship:

  Government budget deficit → Supply of government bonds increases $(GB_s \uparrow)$ → Capacity to buy other bonds decreases → Demand for other bonds decreases → Prices of other bonds fall $(B_p \downarrow)$ → Interest rate rises $(i \uparrow)$

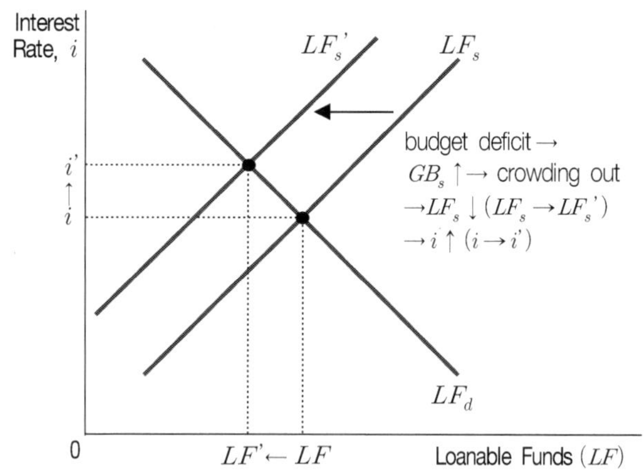

(Week 6)

The Basic Tools of Finance

1. Present Value as a Basic Concept

- **One dollar paid next year has the future value of 1 dollar, which is different from the present 1 dollar.**
  - If you put 1 dollar in a bank account as a deposit, and if the interest rate is i%, then the present 1 dollar will become $1\cdot(1+i)$ dollar in one year.

  - Conversely, if you purchase a bond that pays you 1 dollar next year, then this 1 dollar is the bond's future value.
    - The future value 1 dollar is composed of the present value (PV) and the interest rate (i). One dollar next year $= PV\cdot(1+i)$.
    - Thus, in order to buy a bond that pays 1 dollar next year, we have to subtract the interest to maturity and pay only the present value. This procedure is called discounting:

$$PV\cdot(1+i)=1 \text{ dollar}, \quad PV=\frac{1}{(1+i)}$$

2. Present Value of a Coupon Bond as a General Type

– Concept of a coupon bond

■ A coupon bond pays a fixed amount of interest every term (quarter or year) until maturity, and then pays a specific face amount (F) at maturity.

- A coupon bond is so named because these bonds were in the past issued with detachable coupons. The bond holder would detach a coupon every term and show it to the bond issuer, who would then pay the interest due. Nowadays this coupon interest is paid through transfer to a bank account.
- The fixed interest rate is called the coupon interest rate (i_{cp}), and the coupon income (C) is paid every term in the amount of $C = F \cdot i_{cp}$.
- Because a coupon bond pays fixed interest every term, it is considered a fixed income asset.

– Getting the present value (PV) of the coupon bond

■ The coupon bond cash flow is composed of the coupon income received every term and the face value received at maturity:

$$CF = C + C + C + \cdots + C + F$$

- Every part of the cash flow comes at a different future time. Thus, all of the future cash flows should be converted to present values by discounting based on the interest rate of this coupon bond in the market:

$$PV = C/(1+i)^1 + C/(1+i)^2 + \cdots + C/(1+i)^n + F/(1+i)^n$$

- Yield to maturity: The aforementioned interest rate of the coupon bond (i) equates the total present value of cash flows to the maturity with their value as of today. This is thus called yield to maturity, or the internal rate of return.

- **Implications of the present value (PV) of the coupon bond**

- From the equation of the coupon bond's present value, we can find a very important implication:

$$PV = C/(1+i)^1 + C/(1+i)^2 + \cdots$$

$$
\begin{aligned}
&+C/(1+i)^n+F/(1+i)^n \\
&=C\{1/(1+i)^1+1/(1+i)^2+\cdots \\
&\quad +C/(1+i)^n\}+F/(1+i)^n \\
&=C\cdot\left[\frac{1/(1+i)\{1-1/(1+i)^n\}}{1-1/(1+i)}\right]+\left\{\frac{F}{(1+i)^n}\right\} \\
&=C\cdot\left\{\frac{1}{(1+i)}\cdot\frac{(1+i)}{i}\right\}\cdot\left\{1-\frac{1}{(1+i)^n}\right\} \\
&\quad +\left\{\frac{F}{(1+i)^n}\right\} \\
&=\frac{C}{i}\cdot\left\{1-\frac{1}{(1+i)^n}\right\}+\left\{\frac{F}{(1+i)^n}\right\}
\end{aligned}
$$

$$i_{cp}=C/F,\ C=i_{cp}\cdot F$$

$$
\begin{aligned}
PV&=\frac{i_{cp}\cdot F}{i}\cdot\left\{1-\frac{1}{(1+i)^n}\right\}+\frac{F}{(1+i)^n} \\
&=F\left\{\frac{i_{cp}}{i}-\frac{i_{cp}}{i}\cdot\frac{1}{(1+i)^n}+\frac{1}{(1+i)^n}\right\} \\
&=F\left\{\frac{i_{cp}}{i}+\frac{1}{(1+i)^n}\cdot\left(1-\frac{i_{cp}}{i}\right)\right\}
\end{aligned}
$$

- If $i_{cp} < i$, then $i_{cp}/i < 1$ and $(1-i_{cp}/i) > 0$, and therefore if n increases then $1/(1+i)^n$ decreases and the positive value $1/(1+i)^n\cdot(1-i_{cp}/i)$ decreases.

This means that, if the market interest rate rises to a

level higher than the coupon interest rate, the present value of the coupon bond declines and the bond holder should have a loss.

It also means that the loss of the present value is more extreme the longer the maturity.

- If $i_{cp} > i$, then $i_{cp}/i > 1$ and $(1-i_{cp}/i) < 0$, and therefore if n increases then $1/(1+i)^n$ decreases and the negative value, that is, subtracting value $1/(1+i)^n \cdot (1-i_{cp}/i)$ decreases.

This means that, if the market interest rate falls to a level lower than the coupon interest rate, then the present value of the coupon bond increases and the bond holder should have a gain.

It also means that the gain of the present value is more extreme the longer the maturity.

- If $i_{cp} = i$, then $i_{cp}/i = 1$ and $(1-i_{cp}/i) = 0$, and thus $PV = F$ irrespective of the maturity.

This means that, if the market interest rate equals the coupon interest rate, then the present value of the coupon bond is equal to the face value of the coupon bond.

3. Three Interest Rates of the Coupon Bond

- **Coupon interest rate (i_{cp})**

  - The coupon interest rate (i_{cp}) is fixed when the bond is issued, and this rate is used until maturity. Bond holders receive coupon incomes every term, in the amount of the face value (F) multiplied by this coupon interest rate (i_{cp}): $C = F \cdot i_{cp}$.

- **Yield to maturity (YTM)**

  - The yield to maturity (YTM) is the interest rate which equates the present value of the cash flows and the present value of the bond (PV). In the following equation, the YTM is i:

$$PV = C/(1+i)^1 + C/(1+i)^2 + \cdots + C/(1+i)^n + F/(1+i)^n$$

    - Here, this YTM i is the market interest rate of this coupon bond market. Every kind of coupon bond has its own unique characteristics, depending on its maturity, the financial and risk situation of its issuer, etc. Each coupon bond therefore shows a different market interest rate, which may differ from the overall market interest rate.

– Rate of return

- Concept: The rate of return means the return on the bond during the bond holding period.
  - This rate of return consists of two factors: The first is the difference in the present value between the time of purchase of the bond and the time when it is resold. The second is the coupon income that belongs to the bond holder during the bond holding period.

- Calculation
  - Difference in present values: If we buy a coupon bond at time t at the interest rate i_t, and resell it at time $t+1$ at the interest rate i_{t+1}, then the buying price becomes the following:

$$PV_t = C/(1+i_t)^1 + C/(1+i_t)^2 + \cdots + C/(1+i_t)^n + F/(1+i_t)^n,$$

and the reselling price is as follows:

$$PV_{t+1} = C/(1+i_t)^1 + C/(1+i_t)^2 + \cdots$$
$$+ C/(1+i_{t+1})^{n-1} + F/(1+i_{t+1})^{n-1}$$

The difference during the holding period, ΔPV is the resale price PV_{t+1} - the purchase price $PV_t =$ $= PV_{t+1} - PV_t$.

- Coupon Income: The coupon income $C = F \cdot i_{cp}$ belongs to the bond holder.
- Rate of Return: The rate of return is calculated by the formula (output − input)/input $\times 100(\%)$.

The output is the resale price (PV_{t+1}) + the coupon income (C), and the input is the purchase price (PV_t).

The rate of return is thus {(output − input)/input} $\times 100 = (PV_{t+1} + C - PV_t)/(PV_t) \times 100 = \{(PV_{t+1} - PV_t)/PV_t = C/PV_t\} \times 100$.

Here, when i_{t+1} is lower than i_t, $PV_{t+1} - PV_t$ is positive and the bond holder has a capital gain. When i_{t+1} is higher than i_t, $PV_{t+1} - PV_t$ is negative and the bond holder has a capital loss. $(PV_{t+1} - PV_t)$ $/PV_t$ thus shows the capital gain or loss.

However, the coupon income C is always constant,

and is a current yield.

- Implications of the rate of return: The bond investment strategy should be chosen depending upon the expectation for the interest rate. When the market interest rate is expected to rise due to the central bank's interest rate policy, should the purchase of bonds be increased or decreased?
    - When the market interest rate is expected to rise only once and then remain the same for the time being, a new coupon bond is issued at a new coupon interest rate in reflection of this market expectation.

      Therefore, if we buy a coupon bond at this coupon interest rate there should not be any capital loss since there is no expectation of a further interest rate increase.
    - When the market interest rate is expected to rise several times during a one or two-year period, new coupon bonds will be issued at different new coupon interest rates in reflection of the changing market expectations for the interest rate.

      The coupon interest rates will rise higher and higher. Thus, even bonds with higher coupon interest rates may have some capital losses if the market interest rate rises to an even higher level in the future.

- Let us look at the following example:

  A is the present situation, and the market interest rate is 1.5%. B, C, D and E show that the interest rate is expected to rise by 0.25%p every term.

  If we buy a coupon bond in situation B the coupon interest rate is 1.75%, which is higher than in situation A. But if we hold this bond three more terms until situation E arrives, then the market interest rate should be 2.5% (0.75%p higher than the 1.75% interest rate at the time the bond was purchased). We should have a considerable capital loss.

  Thus, a bond purchase should be decided on in consideration of not only the coupon interest rate, but the expected capital gain or loss due to the future interest rate as well:

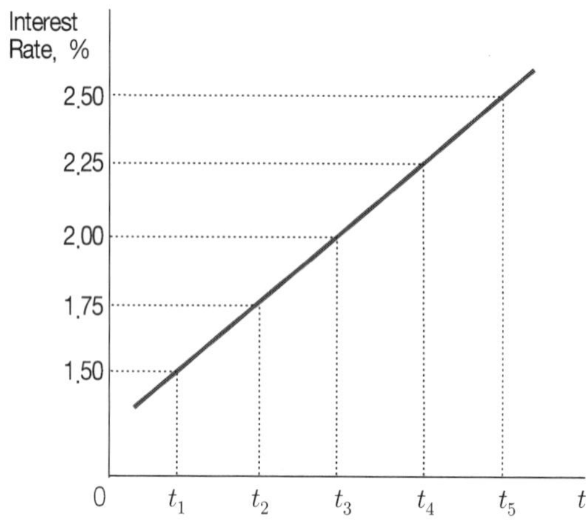

4. Special Issue: Negative Yielding Bonds

– Some cases of negative yielding bonds

- Henkel sold 500 million euros of two-year bonds with a yield of minus 0.05%. Sanofi sold 1 billion euros of three and a half-year bonds with a yield of minus 0.05%. These sales happened in September 2016.

Why would people buy negative yield bonds? There could be three reasons:

- First, if the negative yield bond is less punitive than others, then it is relatively attractive even with a negative yield. If a bank deposit interest rate is lower than −0.05%, for example −0.4%, then this −0.05% coupon bond is relatively better than a bank deposit with a −0.4% interest rate. This is the European situation.
- Second, if the market interest rate is expected to fall from −0.05% to an even lower level, for example −0.3% or −0.4%, then the present value of this −0.05% coupon interest rate bond should increase, resulting in a capital gain.

  Some investors may speculate like this, that the yield of this negative yield bond can fall further to give them a capital gain. They can buy this negative yield bond based on that speculation.
- Third, wealthy persons wish to easily hand down their wealth to their descendants. Giving a large amount of anonymous bonds to their descendants is a convenient and economical way of passing assets on to them.

(Week 7)

The Monetary System

1. The Meaning of Money

- **Money: The term "money" refers to assets that are generally accepted as payment for buying goods and services**
  - Money should have 3 functions: as a medium of exchange, as a unit of account, and as a store of value
  - Money has the highest liquidity among all assets
- **Commodity money and Fiat money**
  - Commodity money: Commodity money is money that is made of precious metals or other valuable commodities, based on their intrinsic values.
  - Fiat money: Fiat money is paper currency decreed by the government to be legal tender. Fiat money is thus not convertible into precious metals.
    - Seigniorage: Seigniorage means the difference between the face value and the intrinsic value of the currency, plus the cost of making it.
    - Origin of the word seigniorage: During the Middle

Ages only the Seignior could mint gold coins, using some gold and announcing a face value higher than the intrinsic value and the minting cost. This difference in value was used to govern the country, and only the Seignior could receive it. The meaning of the word seigniorage originated from that practice.

■ In the debate over the dollar as the key currency and seigniorage, China has argued two points:

- The first is that the dollar, being the national currency of the United States, should not function as the world's key currency. The SDR of the IMF should play that role.
- The second point is that the monopoly of dollar seigniorage by the US is unfair.

Actually, however, the SDR is not adequate for functioning as the key currency. There are no notes and coins in SDRs to be circulated. The IMF also does not have a governing organization that would enable it to function as the world's central bank.

Nominal values and costs of producing the US currency

Denomination	Cost of Production
$1 and $2	5.6 cents per note
$5	11.0 cents per note
$10	11.7 cents per note
$20	10.8 cents per note
$50	12.9 cents per note
$100	13.2 cents per note

Note: 1) As of 2018
Source: US Federal Reserve Board

2. Tools of Monetary Policy

– Conventional Tools of Monetary Policy

- Open Market Operations: The term "open market operations" refers to the purchasing of or selling of bonds by the central bank in the open market.

  - Open market purchases: The central bank purchases bonds from commercial banks, and increases the monetary base in the form of the commercial banks' reserves, which are deposited in the central bank accounts held by the commercial banks.

The central bank can purchase bonds from the non-bank public, by paying them checks. If the public deposits these checks in banks, then the banks' reserves increase. If the public cashes these checks at banks or at the central bank, then the amount of currency in circulation increases.

In summary, when the central bank purchases bonds the monetary base increases in the forms of reserves or of currency in circulation. The monetary base is thus composed of reserves and currency: ($MB = R + C$).

- Open market sales: When the central bank sells bonds to commercial banks or to the public, the monetary base in the forms of reserves or currency decreases.
- Open market operations are implemented with selected primary dealers that satisfy some conditions for serving as dealers.

■ R/P (Repurchasing): The term "R/P" means the borrowing of liquidity by a commercial bank from the central bank, with bonds provided as collateral.

- An R/P is carried out through the selling of bonds first, and repurchasing them later.

- Commercial banks obtain liquidity by selling bonds to the central bank, and return this money by buying back (repurchasing) the bonds later.

  Thus, an R/P is actually a commercial bank's borrowing of some liquidity from the central bank, using bonds as collateral.

- The reverse of an R/P is called a reverse R/P or a matched sale-purchase agreement. Commercial banks buy bonds first and sell them later; the term "matched sale-purchase agreement" reflects the central bank's viewpoint.

■ Required Reserve Ratio (rr)

- The required reserve ratio is the percentage (for example, 5%) of their deposits that commercial banks must keep as reserves in their accounts with the central bank. This amount of deposits cannot be used for lending.
- Changes in the reserve ratio affect the money supply by causing the money multiplier to change.
- A rise in the reserve requirement ratio decreases the room that commercial banks have for lending from their deposits, and results finally in lower money creation due to a decrease in the money multiplier.

- The required reserve ratio is not changed frequently, because of its big impact on the entire banking sector.

■ Discount Policy: Commercial banks sell bonds at discounts, to obtain liquidity from the central bank.

- Commercial banks can obtain some liquidity by selling bonds to the central bank. When a commercial bank sells bonds, the sale value of the bonds is determined by discounting for the remaining period to maturity.

  But these bonds were already discounted when the commercial bank first purchased them. Thus, commercial banks' selling of bonds to the central bank is called rediscounting.

- If the central bank raises the discount interest rate, then the amount of liquidity that commercial banks can obtain by selling their bonds decreases. Thus the demand for discounting also decreases.

- The central bank sets the discount interest rate higher than the target rate, so as to encourage borrowing and lending among commercial banks in the interbank market.

– Unconventional tools of monetary policy

- Concept: In responding to the global financial crisis of 2008, conventional monetary tools faced two limitations. The first was an inability to allocate capital to productive uses. The second was the zero-lower bound interest rate, below which the central bank could not reduce short-term interest rates further.

- Quantitative Easing
  - Central banks including the US Federal Reserve purchased massive quantities of a larger range of bonds than normal, in order to increase the supply of the monetary base.
  - This policy also altered the composition of the Fed's balance sheet and improved credit conditions in some sectors. The central bank can purchase bonds from some particular sector and of some particular maturity, in order to affect liquidity conditions or interest rates in that sector.

B/S of major central banks

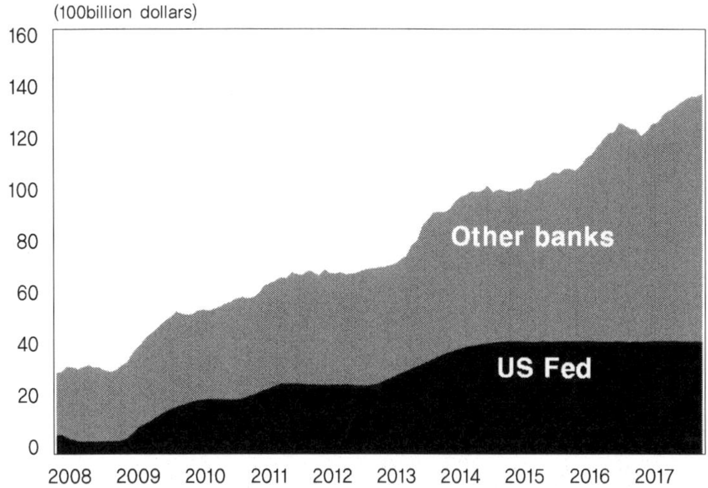

Note: 1) The other banks are the ECB, BOJ and BOE.

B/S of Bank of Korea

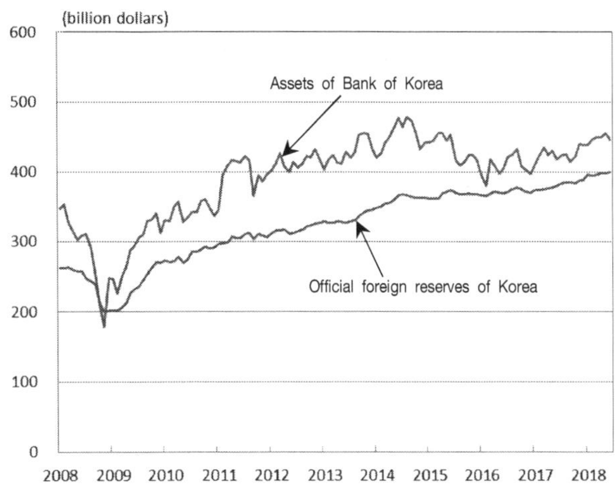

- Forward Guidance
  - The Fed announced a commitment to keep the federal funds rate at zero for a long period of time. This commitment affected the market expectations for future short-term interest rates, and thereby for long-term interest rates as well.
  - Here, the success of forward guidance depends on the credibility of the central bank.

3. The Money Multiplier

– Simple Deposit Multiplier

- When the central bank buys $\$R$ in bonds from a commercial bank, the monetary base increases.

- A commercial bank (Bank 1) can lend $R minus its required reserves. If rr is the required reserve ratio, then it is possible to lend $\$R(1-rr)$ to borrowers.

The borrowers use this money to make payments to other people, and those people then deposit this money in another bank (Bank 2). Bank 2 can lend this $R(1-rr)$ after subtracting its required reserves, and thus $R(1-rr)(1-rr)=R(1-rr)^2$.

This process continues to infinity as follows:

$$\begin{aligned}\Delta D &= R\cdot\left[1+(1-rr)+(1-rr)^2+\cdots\cdots\right]\\ &= R\cdot[1/\{1-(1-rr)\}]\\ &= R\cdot(1/rr)\end{aligned}$$

– The Money Multiplier, extended model

- The monetary base (MB) is composed of the reserves (R) and the currency (C), as we have already seen.
  - The currency is the money that people hold for transactions. How much money of the deposits (D) is held as currency (C) is the currency holding ratio (c). Thus $c=C/D$ and $C=c\cdot D$.
  - The reserves are the money that commercial banks keep in their accounts opened at the central bank in preparation for withdrawals by their depositors.

    Commercial banks maintain reserves in consideration of the required reserve ratio (rr), but at a little higher ratio than the required reserve ratio in order to avoid any possibility of default. This extra reserve money is called excess reserves, and the ratio of these excess reserves over deposits is called the excess reserve ratio (er).

Thus the reserves (R) are composed of the required reserves ($RR = rr \cdot D$) and the excess reserves ($ER = er \cdot D$), and $R = (rr + er) \cdot D$.

- Finally, $MB = C + R = c \cdot D + (rr + er) \cdot D = (c + rr + er) \cdot D$.

■ The money supply is composed of deposits (D) and currency (C).

- When commercial banks lend money, some part of this money is held as currency (C) and the rest returns to the commercial banks as deposits (D).

  Thus $M = C + D = c \cdot D + D = (c + 1) \cdot D$.

– **Using the aforementioned relationships, the money multiplier is derived as follows:**

$$M = m \cdot MB$$

$$C + D = m \cdot (C + R)$$

$$c \cdot D + D = m \cdot \{(c \cdot D) + (rr + er) \cdot D\}$$

$$D(1+c) = m \cdot D(rr + er + c)$$

$$m = (1+c)/(rr + er + c)$$

– Implications of the Money Multiplier

- The money multiplier is composed of three factors, which show the endogeneity or exogeneity of the monetary base and of money:
  - The currency holding ratio (c) is decided largely by the attitudes and preferences of people. The central bank cannot influence the currency holding ratio as it may wish. This means that the currency holding ratio is endogenous rather than exogenous.
  - The required reserve ratio (rr) is decided by the cen- tral bank in reflection of its monetary policy stance. Thus, the required reserve ratio is in general exogen- ous rather than endogenous.
  - The excess reserve ratio (er) is affected by commercial banks' attitudes and strategies. Active and risk-loving commercial banks show low levels of excess reserve ratios, but passive and risk-averse commercial banks maintain relatively high excess reserve ratios.

Thus, an excess reserve ratio is endogenous rather than exogenous.

- **The monetary base is the money supplied by the central bank to commercial banks or to the people. Central banks decide the quantity of the monetary base in reflection of macroeconomic conditions. The monetary base is thus exogenous rather than endogenous.**

  - In an exceptional case of financial crisis, however, the monetary base should be supplied even if the central bank does not wish it. And so it is difficult to say that the monetary base is totally exogenous.

- **Money is composed of currency and deposits.**

  - Currency is largely endogenous because it is decided by the people's currency holding ratios.

  - Deposits are more complicated, however. They are affected by many variables:

    - First, the attitudes of commercial banks, whether aggressive or passive, affect the creation of credit and deposits. If a commercial bank is aggressive, then its excess reserve ratio becomes smaller and the money multiplier becomes larger, resulting in the creation of more money.

- Second, the required reserve ratio is basically decided by the central bank.
- Third, the currency holding ratio is decided naturally by people's attitudes and by social convention.
- Considering these three factors altogether, deposits are much more endogenous than exogenous.

(Week 8)

Money Growth and Inflation

1. Inflation

- **Inflation: Inflation means an increase in the overall level of prices.**
  - Hyperinflation: Hyperinflation means high inflation, exceeding 50% per month.

- **Deflation: Deflation means a decrease in the overall level of prices, and so in a situation of deflation the inflation rate is negative.**
  - Disinflation: Disinflation means that inflation decreases, but is still positive.

- **Inflation Tax: The term "inflation tax" refers to a decrease in purchasing power due to inflation stemming from an increase in the supply of money.**
  - If the central bank increases the printing of money, then inflation rises and the real value of money, i.e. the real purchasing power of the currency, decreases. This is one form of seigniorage income for the central bank.

2. Some Targets of Monetary Policy

– Price Stability

- Definition: Price stability is the final goal of most central banks. Here, price stability means low and stable inflation. Price stability is the most important goal of monetary policy. Why?
  - An unstable rise in the price level causes increased uncertainty in the economy. The decision-making by consumers, businesses and the government for their future plans becomes complicated and difficult.
  - If the central bank manages a stable level of inflation, and if the central bank is credible, then market participants can make long-term future plans in sustainable ways.

- Nominal Anchor and Inflation Targeting: The term "nominal anchor" refers to a nominal variable, such as inflation, that a central bank ties to price stability.
  - Positive effects: First, use of a nominal anchor can limit discretionary monetary policy implementation and promote low and stable inflation expectations.

Second, the central bank can reject requests of the government to join in expansionary monetary policy, citing this nominal anchor.

– High Employment

■ Definition: The goal of high employment is not an unemployment level of zero, but the natural rate of unemployment.

- The natural rate of unemployment is a level above zero, consistent with full employment at which the demand for labor equals the supply of labor.
- A particular level of output is produced at the natural rate of unemployment, and it is referred to as the potential output.

■ We use the natural rate of unemployment due to the following reasons:

- Frictional unemployment, occurring as workers and firms search to find suitable matches with each other, is unavoidable.
- Structural unemployment due to wage rigidity is difficult to eliminate. Wage rigidity is a consequence of

minimum wage laws, labor unions and efficient wages, as we have already seen.

• Appropriate government policy, such as the provision of better information about job vacancies or of job training programs, might lead to a decline in the natural rate of unemployment.

- **Financial Market Stability**

■ Financial crises can weaken the ability of the financial markets to channel funds to productive investment, and lead to sharp contractions in economic activity.

• Stability of the financial system is important in order to avoid financial crises.

- **Interest Rate Stability**

■ Interest rate stability is important for reducing uncertainty in the economy and maintaining stability in the financial markets.

• Interest rate stability is very important for decision-making on long-term investments.

- **Foreign Exchange Market Stability**
  - ■ The stability of the currency is important especially when a country is highly dependent on foreign trade, being a so-called small open economy.
    - A rise in the currency's value lowers the price competitiveness of this country's products.
    - A decrease in its currency's value may enhance the price competitiveness of the country's products, but causes inflation pressures due to the increases in prices of imported goods.

3. Inflation Targeting

- **Concept: Inflation targeting is practiced when the central bank of a country announces a medium-term numerical target for inflation, and also announces an institutional commitment to price stability as a primary goal of its monetary policy.**

- The central bank is thus accountable for the attaining of this inflation target, and its autonomy in monetary policy implementation is respected.

- **Some of the countries that have adopted inflation targeting include New Zealand (1990), Canada (1991), the United Kingdom (1992), Sweden (1993), Finland (1993), Australia (1994) and Spain (1994).**
  - New Zealand adopted a very strict type of inflation target.
    - The Reserve Bank is committed by law to the sole objective of price stability. The Minister of Finance and the Governor of the Reserve Bank should negotiate and make public an agreement on policy targets.
    - This agreement sets out the numerical target range for inflation and the dates for achieving the target. If the targets are not satisfied, then the Governor is subject to dismissal.

- **Advantages of inflation targeting**

  ■ Inflation targeting reduces the likelihood of the central bank pursuing an overly expansionary monetary policy for the sake of short-term performance.

  ■ The central bank can more easily reject political pressures for an expansionary monetary policy, based on its inflation targeting commitment.

  ■ The transparency of policy associated with inflation targeting makes the central bank highly accountable to the public. The central bank's credibility thus rises and its monetary policy can be implemented in a sustainable manner in the long term.

- **Disadvantages of inflation targeting**

  ■ Rigidity: If the central bank implements inflation targeting very rigidly, then it cannot respond appropriately to unforeseen circumstances.

    • This limitation can be overcome by flexible inflation targeting. The central bank can use all available information to determine the most appropriate actions, within a substantial degree of policy discretion.

- Output Fluctuation: If the central bank implements inflation targeting very rigidly, then it should implement a very tight monetary policy that leads to significant fluctuations in output.
  - This problem can be attenuated by medium-term inflation targeting, and by pursuing a gradual reduction of inflation when actual inflation exceeds the target.

4. Monetary Policy Strategy of the US Federal Reserve

– **The Fed of the United States has not articulated any explicit strategy based on a nominal anchor.**

- The Fed uses an implicit nominal anchor in the form of an overriding concern with controlling inflation in the long term.

- The Fed implements preemptive actions against threats of inflation based on careful monitoring for signs of future inflation.

Advantages of the Fed's monetary policy

- The Fed uses the maximum amount of available information to determine the best settings for its monetary policy.
  - The Fed's forward-looking behavior and emphasis on price stability help to discourage adoption of an overly expansionary monetary policy and to ameliorate the time-inconsistency problem.
  - The Fed's monetary policy affects the economies of countries around the world, and the Fed should implement its policy in reflection of the global macroeconomy and global financial conditions also. The present policy approach of the Fed in not using a nominal anchor is therefore reasonable in enabling it to respond to any unforeseen instability in global conditions.

– Disadvantages of the Fed's monetary policy

- Lack of tranparency: Due to the lack of a nominal anchor, Fed watchers make subjective guesses about the Fed's monetary policy stance. There may thus be some overreactions that cause increased instability in the global financial markets.
  - One example of this is the so-called "Bernanke Shock" of 2013. Fed Chair Bernanke signaled only the possibility of the Fed reducing its quantitative easing, depending on whether the US economy improved as expected. Market participants overreacted to this conditional possibility of decreased US quantitative easing, and emerging market stock prices and currencies fell steeply.

- Policy inconsistency: Due to the lack of a nominal anchor, the policy stance of the Fed can be changed based on the preferences of the Fed's chairperson or governors.
  - The Fed can also face political pressures for adoption of an expansionary monetary policy, since there is no nominal anchor.

(Week 9)

Monetary Policy

1. Monetary Policy by Monetary Aggregate Targeting

- **Monetary policy is implemented to secure the final goal of price stability. Central banks thus set intermediate targets for their monetary policies, which should be closely related to price stability, i.e. maintaining the target inflation.**
  - If the central bank can attain its intermediate target, then the final goal of price stability can also be attained. That is the belief of the central bank.
  - There are two possible intermediate targets: a monetary aggregate target, and an interest rate target.

- **Monetary Aggregate Target and Inflation Target**
  - Quantity Theory of Money: Monetary policy that targets a monetary aggregate is based on the quantity theory of money:

    $MV = PT = PY$, taking the natural logarithm

    $\ln(MV) = \ln(PY)$,

$$\ln(M)+\ln(V)=\ln(P)+\ln(Y),\text{ differentiating}$$

$$d\{\ln(M)+\ln(V)\} = d\{\ln(P)+\ln(Y)\}$$

$$(1/M)dM + (1/V)dV = (1/P)dP + (1/Y)dY$$

$$dM/M + dV/V = dP/P + dY/Y$$

$$\dot{M} + \dot{V} = \dot{P} + \dot{Y}$$

$$\dot{M} = \dot{P} + \dot{Y} - \dot{V}$$

where M: the monetary aggregate,
V: the velocity of money,
P: the price level,
T: total transactions in the economy,
Y: the total output of the economy
· over the head means the growth rate

- From the above equation, we have $\dot{M} = \dot{P} + \dot{Y} - \dot{V}$. This equation shows that the targeted amount of increase in the monetary aggregate is the inflation rate plus the GDP growth rate, and minus the increase in the velocity of money circulation.
  - If inflation rises, then the nominal value of the product increases. The money supply should thus also expand, to settle the increased transaction volume.
  - If GDP increases then the money supply should also

increase, to purchase the increased output.

- If the money circulation velocity increases, then the supply of money needed to settle the transaction volume declines. But if the money circulation velocity decreases, then we have to expand the supply of money in order to settle the transaction volume.

■ Classical Dichotomy: The classical school argued that changes in the money supply increase only nominal GDP, but that real GDP does not change in the long run.

- This argument comes from the following reasoning. If the supply of money increases, then this causes the interest rate to decline in the short run, which leads to increases in investment and GDP.

  But in the long run, inflation rises due to the increased supply of money. This inflation causes the real money balance (M/P) to decline, resulting in a higher interest rate. Investment then decreases also, and GDP finally returns to its original level.

– Monetary Aggregate Target and Monetary Base

■ The central bank tries to manage the quantity of the

monetary base using the relationship between the Monetary Base (MB) and the Monetary Aggregate (M) via the Money Multiplier (m):

$$M = m \cdot MB$$

$$M = (1+c)/(rr+er+c) \cdot MB$$

- In using the above equation, the central bank tries to get the best estimates of M, c, rr and er. With these estimates, it tries to control the quantity of MB using its monetary policy tools.
  - If it is estimated that the currency holding ratio (c) will increase, then the money multiplier decreases. The central bank should therefore increase the supply of the monetary base (MB) by purchasing bonds from commercial banks.
  - If it is estimated that the excess reserve ratio (er) will increase, then commercial banks become more conservative in lending and the money multiplier decreases. The central bank should therefore increase the supply of the monetary base (MB) by purchasing bonds from commercial banks.
  - If the central bank needs to increase the monetary

aggregate to achieve the price stability goal (target inflation), then it should consider the equation $M = m \cdot MB$.

If it is estimated that the money multiplier will decrease, then the supply of the monetary base should be increased. But if it is estimated that the money multiplier will increase, then the monetary base should be reduced.

- **In summary, Monetary Policy based on a Monetary Aggregate Target is implemented by analyses of two linkages:**
  - The first is the linkage between the monetary aggregate and the final price stability target (the inflation target).
  - The second is the linkage between the monetary base and the monetary aggregate, simultaneously with the linkage between the money multiplier and the monetary aggregate.

2. Monetary Policy by Interest Rate Targeting

– Interest Rate Target and Inflation Target

- At present, almost all central banks adopt interest rate targeting monetary policies. They try to maintain benchmark interest rates within certain ranges, which show the degrees of interest rate stability that they target.

- This policy comes from the belief that the stability of interest rates is very closely related to the stability of prices.

– Implementation of Interest Rate Targeting Monetary Policy

- Selecting the benchmark interest rate of a Target Interest Rate Level or Zone

  - The central bank chooses the benchmark interest rate for its monetary policy. This interest rate should show well the short-term liquidity situation of commercial banks.

If this interest rate rises to a level higher than the central bank's target, then the central bank should increase the supply of the monetary base by purchasing bonds from commercial banks.

If it falls to a level lower than the target, then the central bank should reduce the supply of the monetary base by selling bonds to commercial banks.

- The US Federal Reserve monitors the federal funds rate (ff) as its benchmark interest rate.

  Here, the federal funds rate (ff) means the interest rate that Fed member banks pay for short-term borrowings from other Fed member banks to comply with the Fed's required reserve (rr) ratio.

  Thus, the federal funds rate (ff) shows the real-time liquidity situation of the Fed member banks.

■ Setting of Target Interest Rate by the Fed: The Fed sets the federal funds target rate as follows (Taylor Rule):

$$FF_{target} = \text{inflation rate} + \text{equilibrium real } FF \text{ rate} + 1/2(\text{inflation gap}) + 1/2(\text{output gap})$$

- First, the Fed sets the real federal funds target rate ($FF_{target}-$ inflation rate) based on the equilibrium real FF rate:

  $FF_{target}-$ inflation rate $=$ equilibrium real FF rate

  But the real federal funds target rate is actually an ex ante concept, and in implementing its monetary policy the Fed sets the nominal federal funds target rate:

  $FF_{target}=$ inflation rate $+$ equilibrium real FF rate

- And if the economy deviates from its long-term equilibrium level, then the FF_{target} rate should be changed in reflection of this deviation.

  If inflation is higher than the target, i.e. if the inflation gap (inflation − target inflation) is positive, then the FF_{target} rate should be raised with the coefficient of 1/2.

  If inflation is lower than the target, i.e. if the inflation gap (inflation − target inflation) is negative, then the FF_{target} rate should be lowered with the coefficient of 1/2.

- Implication of positive value 1/2 coefficient:

Let us try to find the implications of this Taylor Rule, under the following assumptions: ① an equilibrium real FF rate of 2%, ② target inflation of 2%, and ③ an output gap of 1%.

If inflation rises from the 2% target level to 3%, then how should the FF_{target} rate be changed?

$$FF_{target,\,\pi=2\%} = \text{inflation rate } (2\%) + \text{equilibrium real } FF \text{ rate } (2\%) + 1/2(\text{inflation gap, } 0\%) + 1/2(\text{output gap, } 1\%) = 4.5\%$$

$$FF_{target,\,\pi=2\%} = \text{inflation rate } (3\%) + \text{equilibrium real } FF \text{ rate } (2\%) + 1/2(\text{inflation gap, } 1\%) + 1/2(\text{output gap, } 1\%) = 6.0\%$$

The difference is 6.0−4.5=1.5%p. This means that, if inflation deviates from the target by 1%p, then the FF_{target} rate should be raised by 1.5%p. This is because the FF_{target} rate should be raised in real interest rate terms in order to reduce inflation. In order to raise the real interest rate, the nominal interest rate should be raised to a level higher than the inflation rate.

- Meaning of the Fed's Taylor Rule: The Taylor Rule is useful as a guide to monetary policy. But the Fed does not follow the Taylor Rule automatically.

  This is because there is no perfect model of the economy, and because even the best economist does not know the current inflation gap and output gap with certainty at any given moment.

3. From Monetary Aggregate Targeting Monetary Policy to Interest Rate Targeting Monetary Policy

– In the past, central banks adopted monetary aggregate targeting monetary policies. But at present almost all central banks have adopted interest rate targeting policies.

Why have central banks shifted from monetary

aggregate targeting to interest rate targeting policies?

- Limitations of monetary aggregate targeting monetary policy
  - Unclear linkage: The two linkages that a monetary aggregate targeting monetary policy is based on have become weaker and weaker.

    First, the linkage of $MV=PY$, and of $\dot{M}=\dot{P}+\dot{Y}-\dot{V}$ have become unclear. Obtaining the inflation and GDP data is only possible after a long time lag, and it is also difficult to obtain accurate data.

    Second, the linkage of $MB \cdot m = M$ is also becoming increasingly weaker. The components of the money multiplier, especially the currency holding ra- tio (c) and the excess reserve ratio (er), are basic- ally endogenous variables. It is thus difficult for the central bank to estimate them correctly to reflect the actual situation.
  - Time lag of monetary policy: If the central bank implements monetary policy based on an evaluation of the economic situation, it takes a long time for the policy to show its effects. And by the time the central bank sees the effects of its monetary policy,

the economic situation may have already changed.

- Relative superiority of the interest rate target compared to the monetary aggregate target
  - Real-time monitoring: The central bank can monitor in real time the movements of market interest rates. All kinds of nominal interest rates are checked by the central bank in real time, and the central bank can immediately see whether some interest rate policy measures are necessary or not.
  - Various tools: The central bank can evaluate the movements of the different market interest rates. It can thus select some precise policy measures focusing on some particular sectors or some particular bond maturities.

Let us consider two examples:

The first example is Operation Twist, carried out by the US Federal Reserve.

After the global financial crisis in 2008 the Fed lowered the target interest rate, expecting that market interest rates would follow and decline as well. But market interest rates, especially long-term rates, did not fall enough.

The Fed therefore purchased long-term bonds in order to reduce long-term interest rates, while selling short-term bonds to keep the money supply neutral (i.e. the increase in the monetary base due to the Fed's purchases of long-term bonds was neutralized by the Fed's selling of short-term bonds that reduced the monetary base.)

Here the selling of short-term bonds might have pushed short-term interest rates up, but this rise in short-term interest rates was not serious due to the lowering of the short-term target interest rate by the Fed.

The second example is the so-called "Yield Curve Control (YCC)" of the Bank of Japan (BOJ).

After the introduction of Abenomics, Japanese market interest rates were in general almost as low as zero. The difference between the short-term and the long-term interest rates, i.e. the interest rate spread $(i_{long\ term} - i_{short\ term})$ approached zero. This interest rate spread is the main source of banking sector profits. In order to widen this spread, the BOJ needed to either raise long-term rates or lower short-term rates.

But Abenomics is basically a policy of increasing the monetary supply to get out of deflation. Thus the BOJ could not sell long-term bonds, which would push long-term interest rates up. The BOJ had to buy short-term bonds, in oder to make short-term interest rates fall. A wider interest rate spread was helpful for the banking sector of Japan.

Monetary Policy Transmission Mechanism

$$MB \cdot m = M$$

$$m = \left(\frac{1+c}{rr+er+c} \right)$$

$$MV = PY$$

$$\dot{M} = \dot{P} + \dot{Y} - \dot{V}$$

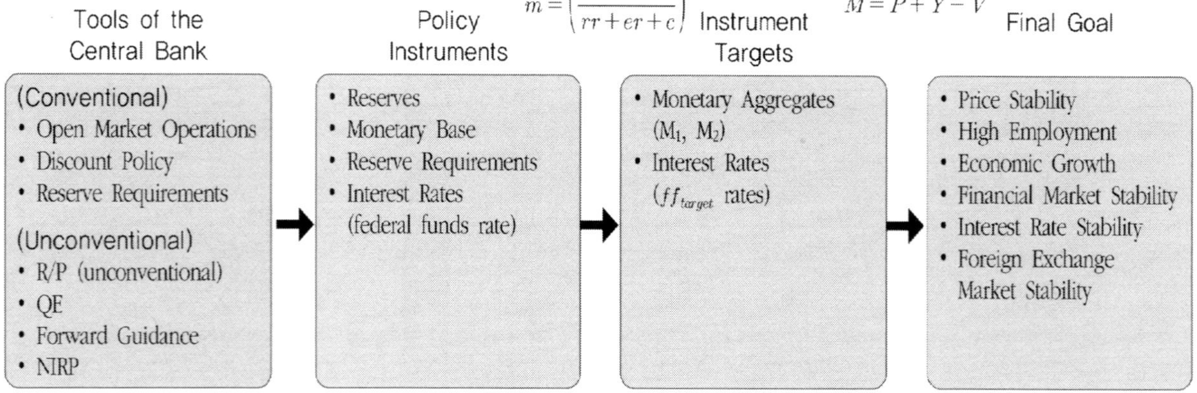

e.g.) open market purchases $\rightarrow MB \uparrow \rightarrow M \uparrow \rightarrow \dot{P} \uparrow$

open market sales $\rightarrow MB \downarrow \rightarrow M \downarrow \rightarrow \dot{P} \downarrow$

$ff_{target} \downarrow \rightarrow ST_i \downarrow \rightarrow LT_i \downarrow \rightarrow \dot{P} \uparrow$

$ff_{target} \uparrow \rightarrow ST_i \uparrow \rightarrow LT_i \uparrow \rightarrow \dot{P} \downarrow$

(Week 10)

International Economics I

1. Concept of Exchange Rate

- **The exchange rate is the price in the foreign exchange market. The foreign exchange (FX) market is the place where different currencies are traded.**

    - The foreign exchange (FX) market is also a market in which a currency's price is determined by the equilibrium between the demand for and the supply of that currency.

- **Spot FX market and Forward FX market**

    - Spot FX market: In the spot FX market, settle- ments of trades are carried out within two business days after they are done. This means that the settle- ments are done either on the trading day (t), on the next business day after the trade ($t+1$), or on the second business day after the trade ($t+2$).

        - By market practice, interbank spot trading is settled on business day $t+2$, as long as there are no special conditions involved.
        - But if there are special conditions, even interbank spot trading can be settled on business days t or

$t+1$. In this case settlement is done ahead of the market practice settlement date, and the settlement amount should be discounted for this settlement carried out ahead of time.

- Forward FX market: In the forward FX market, settlements are done later than two business days after trading, i.e. from the third business day after the trading day ($\sim t+3$).
  - The forward exchange rate is composed of the spot exchange rate + interest for this delay in settlement. This interest is referred to as swap points. Thus the forward exchange rate is the spot exchange rate + the swap points.

– Cross exchange rate and Arbitrage exchange rate

- Calculating the arbitrage exchange rate: The arbitrage exchange rate is calculated using two other existing market exchange rates.
  - If there is no foreign exchange market for trading between two currencies, for example between the Japanese Yen and the Korean Won, then it is not possible to find a market exchange rate between

them. In this case we can calculate the Won/Yen exchange rate using the arbitrage mechanism:

(Won/dollar)/(Yen/dollar) → Won/Yen

- We can use the existing market Won/dollar and Yen/dollar exchange rates to calculate the Won/Yen rate. Here the two exchange rates, the Won/dollar and the Yen/dollar, are crossed in order to get the Won/Yen exchange rate. Thus these two exchange rates, the Won/dollar and the Yen/dollar, are called the cross exchange rates used to obtain the arbitrage Won/Yen exchange rate.

■ Adverse effect of arbitrage exchange rate: This arbitrage exchange rate has a distorting effect on the exchange rate.

- We use the relationship (Won/Yen) = (Won/dollar) /(Yen/dollar). If the Yen/dollar exchange rate rises, then the arbitrage Won/Yen exchange rate falls. This is because the rise in the denominator {(Yen/dollar) ↑} causes a decrease in the exchange rate (Won/Yen) = {(Won/dollar)/(Yen/dollar) ↑} ↓.

  This means that a depreciation of the Yen against the dollar, due to Abenomics for example, causes

Won appreciation against the Yen.

- If there were a foreign exchange market for trading between the Won and the Yen, then this Won appreciation against the Yen seen by using the arbitrage mechanism would not happen.

– Nominal, Real, Nominal Effective and Real Effective Exchange Rates, and dollar Index

■ Nominal Exchange Rate: The nominal exchange rate is the exchange rate that we see in our ordinary lives. If there is no special indication, then the exchange rate we talk about is the nominal exchange rate.

- The nominal exchange rate is denoted as follows:

$$E = \text{Won/dollar or dollar/Euro}$$

- The US dollar (dollar) is the key currency, and the values of other currencies are denoted against the dollar. The dollar is thus located in the denominator.
- There are some exceptions to this, however. The Euro and the Pound Sterling are located in the denominators even against the dollar.

■ Real Exchange Rate: In economics, the real value is

the nominal value deflated by the price. We obtain the real exchange rate also by deflating the nominal exchange rate by the price of each currency concerned.

- The real exchange rate is denoted as follows:

$$RE = (\text{Won}/P_{Won})/(\text{dollar}/P_{dollar})$$

- Effective Exchange Rate: The exchange rate is a very important factor affecting the net exports (exports−imports) of a country. In line with this, we need to calculate an exchange rate against the currencies of our major trading partner countries. The changes of these currencies' values affect our trade balance.
  - The nominal effective exchange rate is calculated using the nominal exchange rates of the currencies of our major trading partner countries.
  - The real effective exchange rate is calculated using the real exchange rates of the currencies of our major trading partner countries.
- Effective Exchange Rate Index: In general, when we denote an exchange rate we put the dollar in the denominator and the other currency in the numerator

(except in certain special cases like those of the Euro and the Pound Sterling). Thus, to make comparisons possible, we put all of the currencies being compared in the denominator.

We give the same starting point value of 100 to each currency, and compare whether the values of the different currencies rise or fall through this index. If a currency's index value is over 100, then the currency has appreciated. If it is under 100, the currency has depreciated.

- The nominal effective exchange rate index (NEERI) is calculated using the nominal exchange rates of the different currencies.
- The real effective exchange rate index (REERI) is calculated by deflating the NEERI by the purchasing power parity index (PPI):

$$NEERI = \frac{\pi(ER_{it}/ER_{io})^{W_{it}}}{(KER_t/KER_o)} \times 100$$

$$= \pi(WER_{it}/WER_{io})^{W_{it}} \times 100$$

$$REERI = \frac{NEERI}{PPI} \times 100$$

$$PPI = \frac{\pi(FPI_{it}/FPI_{io})^{W_{it}}}{(KPI_t/KPI_o)} \times 100$$

$$= \pi \frac{(FPI_{it}/KPI_t)^{W_{it}}}{(FPI_{io}/KPI_o)^{W_{it}}} \times 100$$

where W_i: trade weight of country i,
ER_i: exchange rate of currency i against the dollar,
KER: exchange rate of Korean Won against the dollar,
WER: exchange rate of currency i against the Korean Won,
FPI_i: price index of country i,
KPI: price index of Korea,
subscript t: comparison timing,
subscript o: basis timing

- dollar Index: The dollar Index is an index of the US dollar's value relative to a basket of foreign currencies.
  - It is a weighted geometric mean of the dollar's value relative to those of other selected currencies. The weights of the currencies are as follows: Euro 57.6%, Japanese Yen 13.6%, Pound Sterling 11.9%, Canadian dollar 9.1%, etc.
  - The dollar Index was launched in March 1973 with a value of 100. If this value rises then it means an appreciation of the dollar since that time.

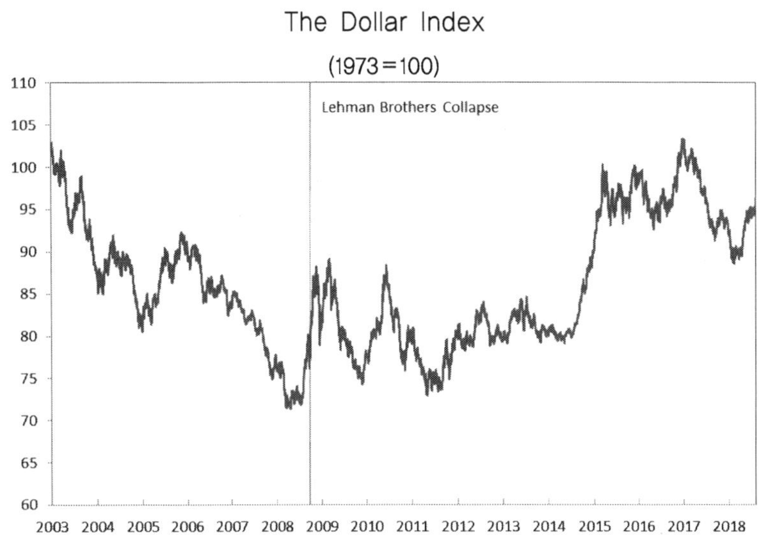

2. Evaluation of the Exchange Rate

– Under free-floating exchange rate regime: Depreciation and Appreciation

- Depreciation: Depreciation means a decline in a currency's value through the market mechanism. If the supply of a currency in the foreign exchange market increases, while the demand for this currency remains unchanged, then the value of the currency falls. This is depreciation, a decrease in the price of a currency in the market.

- Appreciation: Appreciation means a rise in a currency's value through the market mechanism. If the demand for a currency in the foreign exchange market increases, while the supply of this currency is unchanged, then the currency's value rises. This is appreciation, an increase in the price of a currency in the market.

- **Under fixed exchange rate regime: Devaluation and Revaluation**

- Devaluation: Devaluation is a decrease in the value of a currency due to artificial and intentional actions of the foreign exchange authority. The authority announces a change of its fixed exchange rate made in order to lower the value of the national currency.

- Revaluation: A revaluation is an increase in a currency's value through the artificial and intentional action of the foreign exchange authority. The authority announces a change of its fixed exchange rate made so as to raise the value of the national currency.

Examples of Evaluation of Exchange Rate Level

■ Nominal exchange rate

- If the exchange rate between the Korean Won and the US dollar, i.e. the Won/dollar rate, rises, then in order to buy 1 dollar it is necessary to pay more Won than previously. This means an appreciation of the dollar and a depreciation of the Won, in terms of their nominal exchange rate.
- If the Won/dollar exchange rate falls, then in order to buy 1 dollar payment of less Won than before is required. This means a depreciation of the dollar and an appreciation of the Won, in terms of their nominal exchange rate.

■ Real exchange rate

- If the real exchange rate of the Korean Won against the US dollar, i.e. $\{(Won/P_{Won})/(dollar/P_{dollar})\}$, rises, then the real value of the dollar rises and the real value of the Won falls.
- If the real exchange rate of the Korean Won against the US dollar, i.e. $\{(Won/P_{Won})/(dollar/P_{dollar})\}$, falls, then the real value of the dollar declines and

the real value of the Won rises.

- Nominal and Real exchange rates: Let us look at the nominal exchange rate and the real exchange rate together.
  - The real exchange rate of the Korean Won against the US dollar is as follows:

$$RE = \{(\text{Won}/P_{Won})/(\text{dollar}/P_{dollar})\}$$
$$= \{(\text{Won}/\text{dollar})/(P_{Won}/P_{dollar})\}$$
$$RE = E/(P_{Won}/P_{dollar}) = E \cdot (P_{dollar}/P_{Won})$$
$$\dot{RE} = \{E \cdot (\dot{P}_{dollar}/P_{Won})\}$$
$$\dot{RE} = \dot{E} + \dot{P}_{dollar} - \dot{P}_{Won}$$

  - If the nominal exchange rate (E) rises by 2%, the US inflation is 3% and the Korean inflation 5% (Korean inflation 2%p higher than that of the US), then the depreciation of the nominal exchange rate equals the difference in inflation between the two countries.

    Thus the two countries' currencies have exactly the same purchasing powers even after inflation, and the relative purchasing power parity holds.

Let us look at a numerical example, assuming that Korea and the US produce exactly the same product A.

In year t (Y_t), the nominal Won/dollar exchange rate is 1,000 $(E=1{,}000)$, the Korean price of product A is 1,000 Won $(P_{A,\,Korea}=1{,}000$ Won$)$, and the US price of product A is 1 dollar $(P_{A,\,USA}=1$ dollar$)$:

$$E=1{,}000,$$
$$P_{A,\,Korea}=1{,}000 \text{ Won},$$
$$P_{A.\,USA}=1 \text{ dollar}$$

In year $t+1$ (Y_{t+1}), the nominal Won/dollar exchange rate is 1,020 $(E=1{,}020)$, the Korean price of product A is 1,050 Won $(P_{A,\,Korea}=1{,}050$ Won$)$, and the US price of product A is 1.03 dollar $(P_{A,\,USA}=$ 1.03 dollar$)$:

$$E=1{,}020,$$
$$P_{A,\,Korea}=1{,}050 \text{ Won},$$
$$P_{A.\,USA}=1.03 \text{ dollar}$$

Converting the Korean price to US dollar terms, $P_{A,\,Korea}=1{,}050$ Won $=1{,}050/1{,}020=1.0294$ dollar $\fallingdotseq$ 1.03 dollar, and so the Korean price is almost the same as the US price. Thus the relative purchasing power parity holds, and the prices of this product in Korea and in the US are equal.

- If the nominal exchange rate (E) rises by 5%, and inflation is 3% in the US and 5% in Korea (the Korean inflation is 2%p higher than that of the US), then the depreciation of the nominal exchange rate (5%) is 3%p higher than the difference in inflation between the two countries.

  The Korean Won thus depreciates by 3% in terms of the real exchange rate.

Let us consider a numerical example, assuming that Korea and the US produce exactly the same product A.

In year t (Y_t), the nominal Won/dollar exchange rate is 1,000 (E=1,000), the Korean price of product A is 1,000 Won ($P_{A,\,Korea}$ = 1,000 Won), and the US price of product A is 1 dollar ($P_{A,\,USA}$ = 1 dollar):

$$E = 1{,}000,$$

$$P_{A,\,Korea} = 1{,}000 \text{ Won},$$

$$P_{A.\,USA} = 1 \text{ dollar}$$

In year $t+1$ (Y_{t+1}), the nominal Won/dollar exchange rate is 1,050 ($E=1,050$), the Korean price of product A is 1,050 Won ($P_{A,\,Korea}=1,050$ Won), and the US price of product A is 1.03 dollar.

Converting the Korean price to US dollar terms, $P_{A,\,Korea}=1,050$ Won$=1,050/1,050=1.00$ dollar. The Korean price of 1.00 dollar is 3% lower than the US price of 1.03 dollar. The depreciation of the Korean Won by 3% in terms of the real exchange rate means that the price of the product becomes 3% cheaper in Korea than it is in the US in dollar terms. The price competitiveness of the Korean good thus rises by 3%.

- If the nominal exchange rate (E) rises by 1% (1% depreciation), inflation is 3% in the US and 5% in Korea (the Korean inflation is 2%p higher than that of the US), then the depreciation of the nominal exchange rate (1%) is by 1%p less than the difference in their inflation levels.

  The Korean Won thus appreciates by 1% in real exchange rate terms.

Let us consider a numerical example, assuming that Korea and the US produce exactly the same product A. In year t (Y_t), the nominal Won/dollar exchange rate is 1,000 ($E=1{,}000$), the Korean price of product A is 1,000 Won ($P_{A,\,Korea}=1{,}000$ Won), and the US price of product A is 1 dollar ($P_{A,\,USA}=1$ dollar):

$$E=1{,}000,$$

$$P_{A,\,Korea}=1{,}000 \text{ Won},$$

$$P_{A.\,USA}=1 \text{ dollar}$$

In year $t+1$ (Y_{t+1}), the nominal Won/dollar exchange rate is 1,010 ($E=1{,}010$), the Korean price of product A is 1,050 Won ($P_{A,\,Korea}=1{,}050$ Won), and the US price of product A is 1.03 dollar ($P_{A,\,USA}=$ 1.03 dollar).

Converting the Korean price to US dollar terms, $P_{A,\,Korea}=1{,}050$ Won $=1{,}050/1{,}010=1.04$ dollar. The Korean price of 1.04 dollar is 1% higher than the US price of 1.03 dollar. The 1% appreciation of the Korean Won in real exchange rate terms means that the price of the product has become 1% more expensive in Korea than it is in the US in dollar terms. Thus the price competitiveness of the product made in Korea falls by 1%.

Here we see that, even with a depreciation of the nominal exchange rate, the real exchange rate can appreciate.

- If the NEER and REER Indexes of a currency rise, then the value of the currency rises by definition, since the changes of this currency are located in the denominator, as the dollar Index.

3. Determinants of the Exchange Rate

$$E = f(M, \pi, Y, i - i^{*}, CA, KA, Psy, \cdots)$$

– Monetary supply and Inflation

- If the monetary supply of a country expands, then the price level of this country should rise. The value of this country's currency should thus fall in nominal terms due to the resulting inflation. This means a depreciation of the country's currency in terms of its nominal exchange rate.

- If the depreciation of the nominal exchange rate is lower than the inflation rate, then the currency shows an appreciation in real exchange rate terms.

- **GDP data (see Week 1)**
- **Interest rate differential: If a country's interest rate rises while other countries' interest rates remain constant, then the interest rate differentials between them increase. We should consider the effects of this increase in the interest rate differential not only through the bond market channel but also through the equity market channel.**

  - Bond market channel: In the bond market, a rise in interest rates has two different effects. The first is an increase in coupon interest income. The second is potential future capital gain or loss possibilities.

    - If the interest rate is expected to rise only once and

then remain the same for the time being, then the newly issued coupon bonds will pay a coupon interest rate reflecting this expectation. But a capital loss is not expected because a further rise in the interest rate is not anticipated. There will thus be some inflow of capital to the bond market of this country.

- If the interest rate is expected to rise several times during some period, then the newly issued coupon bonds will pay higher coupon interest rates than now, but potential capital losses can be expected because further rises in the interest rate are anticipated. Before deciding on their investments, investors will thus analyze the net benefits of this positive coupon income as well as the possible negative capital losses.

■ Equity market channel: In the equity market, a rise in interest rates has two different effects. The first is a rise in the borrowing costs of firms. The second is a positive evaluation of this country's economy by foreigners.

- If the interest rate is expected to rise, then the

borrowing costs of firms increase. This is a negative factor for the values of equities, and there should thus be some outflows of capital.

- But if foreigners evaluate the economy of this country positively due to the rise in its interest rate, then they may increase their purchases of this country's equities and inflows of capital are possible.

  This situation is possible when a rise in interest rates is forecast due to expectations of monetary policy tightening in a country. If foreigners accept the monetary tightening of the central bank as a signal that the central bank is confident about the country's economy, then they will buy the equities of this country.

– Limitations of Empirical Tests

■ An increase of the foreign-domestic interest rate differential causes an appreciation of the national currency, the Korean Won for example. But sometimes the empirical tests do not show any statistically significant causality for this. Why?

- Offsetting effects of bond market and equity market channels:

If the interest rate differential increases in Korea, then there may be inflows of foreign capital to the Korean bond market, if capital losses are not expected. This is a factor causing appreciation of the Korean Won.

But an increase in the interest rate differential may have negative effects on the Korean equity market, due to the rising costs of firms. There may be outflows of foreign capital from the Korean equity market.

The aforementioned two opposite directional effects offset each other, and the final result may not be significant statistically.

- This is because we cannot separate the effect of the interest rate differential in the exchange rate on the bond market from that on the equity market.

- **Current Account and Capital Account: Capital inflows through the current and capital accounts cause increased demand for the currency, and the currency should thus appreciate.**

■ The current account is due mainly to exports and imports, i.e. net exports.

   - If a country's net exports grow, then the surplus of its current account expands and inflows of the dollar increase. These dollar inflows should be converted to this country's national currency, and the resulting sales of dollars and buying of the national currency cause the dollar to depreciate and the national currency to appreciate.

- The capital account is due to the inflows of foreign capital investment.
   - The first type of this investment is foreigners' investment in the country's firms to produce goods and to participate in these firms' management. This is called foreign direct investment (FDI). FDI is an investment in firms and is thus long-term investment. FDI is therefore not volatile in the short run.
   - The second type of foreign capital inflows in the capital account is portfolio investment to purchase bonds and equities. If the returns of bonds or equities are lower than the investor's targets, then the investors may withdraw their funds. Portfolio investment is thus more volatile than FDI in the short run.

- Inflows of capital through FDI or portfolio investment cause appreciation of the national currency, and outflows of capital (or repatriation, as it is called in market jargon) cause the national currency to depreciate.

■ Is a deficit in the current account always covered by a surplus in the capital account?

- If a country's current account deficit is not serious, then this country can borrow foreign capital and cover the deficit in its current account by the surplus in its capital account.
- But if a country's current account deficit is serious, and if a large deficit continues, then the country cannot easily borrow foreign capital. The credibility of this country deteriorates and its borrowing from abroad becomes more and more difficult.

  In this case, the country's foreign reserve assets should be used to pay the current account deficit. If the foreign reserve assets are not sufficient, then this country may have to request emergency liquidity from the IMF (International Monetary Fund). When receiving IMF liquidity, the country will have to respect the policy recommendations of the IMF. It will therefore be giving up its monetary policy sovereignty.

- **Political factors**

  - Geopolitical tensions: If geopolitical tensions increase, then market participants become more conservative and prefer safer assets. In the foreign exchange market, the dollar is one of the safe currencies, and when geopolitical tensions increase the demand for the dollar grows and the dollar appreciates.

  - International political accords: The so-called Group of 5 (G5) finance ministers agreed on appreciations of the German Mark and the Japanese Yen in 1985, in the so-called Plaza Accord. And after that the German Mark and the Japanese Yen appreciated:

    - If there were another international political accord similar to the Plaza Accord, then it should affect foreign exchange rate trends in the medium to long term.

– Debate over Safe Currency

- Concept of Safe Currency: A safe currency means a currency whose value rises due to an increase in demand when risk increases in the international financial markets. The dollar and the Japanese Yen are typical examples of safe currencies.

  - As the world's key currency, the dollar is the most typical example of a safe currency. After World War II the dollar became the key currency of the world, with the value of gold coming to be expressed in units of dollars.

The values of gold for other currencies should be calculated by the exchange rates between those currencies and the dollar.

- The Yen is also a safe currency, whose value rises when market participants become risk averse. The Yen is different from the dollar, however. The Yen's use is a typical example of the so-called carry trade.

  Due to the long-lasting low interest rates under the deflationary circumstances in Japan, the Yen has been used in the carry trade. When the global economy has been expected to grow faster, then investors have purchased higher return, riskier assets. They have borrowed Yen at very low interest rates and invested it in assets having higher expected returns, Australian assets for example. Borrowing the Yen at 0.5% and investing it in Australian assets at 3.0% means a 2.5% expected return, if we neglect the effects of any changes in the exchange rate. This is called the carry trade.

  If market sentiment reverses, then investors unwind their carry trades, selling Australian dollars and buying Yen. In this case the Yen can appreciate steeply, sometimes more steeply than the US dollar.

- If the Yen appreciates faster than the dollar, then does this mean that the Yen is safer than the dollar?
  - If the investors sold the dollar and purchased the Yen, then we could say yes. But if the rapid Yen appreciation were due to the unwinding of carry trades, then we could not say yes.

(Week 11)

International Economics II

4. Exchange Rate Regime

- **Concept: The term "exchange rate regime" refers to the type of exchange rate management, i.e. whether the exchange rate is fixed by the authority or allowed to float in the foreign exchange market. A country chooses between a Fixed Exchange Rate Regime and a Free-floating Exchange Rate Regime.**

  - Fixed exchange rate regime: In a fixed exchange rate regime, the value of the currency is pegged relative to the value of another currency. The exchange rate is thus fixed in terms of the anchor currency.

    - For example, the Hong Kong dollar (HK$) is pegged to the US dollar (dollar), and trades within a tight range of HK$7.75 to HK$7.85 against the dollar.

  - Free-floating exchange rate regime: In a free-floating exchange rate regime, the value of a currency is allowed to fluctuate against those of all other currencies.

  - Managed floating exchange rate regime: If the authorities operating a floating exchange rate regime intervene in the foreign exchange market to influence the exchange rate by purchasing and selling foreign currencies, then the regime is referred to as a managed floating exchange rate regime or a dirty floating exchange rate regime.

Exchange rate arrangements

Classifications		Number of countries
[Hard pegs]	No separate legal tenders, Currency boards	25 (Hong Kong SAR, Ecuador, etc.)
[Soft pegs]	Conventional pegs, Crawling pegs, Bands	76 (China, Vietnam, Czech Rep., etc.)
[Floating]	Free-floating, Floating	71 (EMU, Australia, Korea, Indonesia, etc.)

Notes: 1) As of December 2016
Source: IMF(2016)

- **Vulnerability to speculative attack: What type of exchange rate regime is more vulnerable to a speculative attack?**
  - Fixed exchange rate regime: In a fixed exchange rate regime, the value of the currency is maintained within a narrow range.

- Therefore, if a speculative attack to weaken the currency's value occurs, then the authority has to sell the dollar and buy its own nation's currency to maintain the exchange rate within the officially announced range.
- Selling the dollar means a reduction in the foreign reserves. If the speculative attack continues, then due to its limited quantity of foreign reserve assets the country cannot continue selling dollars to support its exchange rate. At some time in the future this country's foreign reserve assets will be exhausted.
- A fixed exchange rate regime is thus vulnerable to speculative attacks in line with the limits of its foreign reserves.

■ Free-floating exchange rate regime: In a free-floating exchange rate regime, the value of the currency is allowed to fluctuate against those of all other currencies.

- Therefore, in the case of a speculative attack to weaken the currency's value, the authority has no need to sell the dollar so as to maintain the exchange rate but just lets the currency depreciate.

- One important point here is that the speculator also takes on exchange rate risk. Even if the currency depreciates as the speculator intends, the currency can revert to appreciation at any time due to other factors involved in the free-floating exchange rate regime. If the magnitude of the appreciation is greater than that of the depreciation, then this speculator loses money. A free-floating exchange rate regime is less vulnerable to speculative attacks.

– Impossible Trinity

■ Concept: The term "Impossible Trinity" refers to the fact that a country cannot pursue at the same time all three of the following policies: ① free capital mobility, ② a fixed exchange rate, and ③ an independent monetary policy.

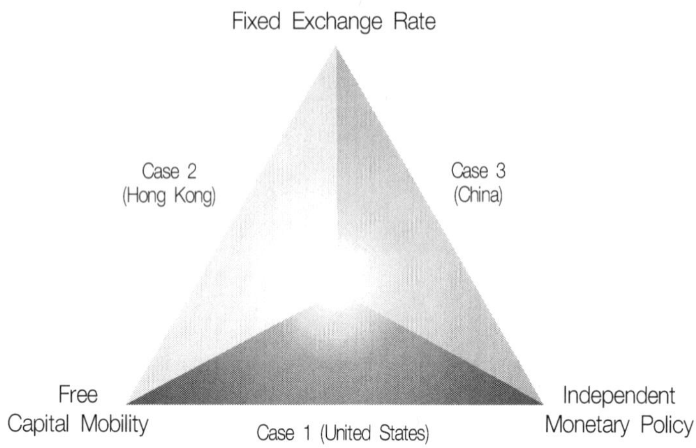

■ Interpretation of three cases

- Case I: The US has selected the policies of ① free capital mobility and ③ an independent monetary policy, giving up ② a fixed exchange rate.

  Due to its free capital mobility, capital inflows to and outflows from the US are always possible, and they change the value of the dollar.

  If the US wanted a fixed exchange rate, then the Fed would have to intervene in the foreign exchange market to neutralize the inflows or outflows of capital, which would mean that monetary policy was dependent on these capital flows. But here the US has given up having a fixed exchange rate and chosen an independent monetary policy.

- Case II: Hong Kong has chosen to have ① free capital mobility and ② a fixed exchange rate, and given up ③ an independent monetary policy.

  Due to its free capital mobility, inflows and outflows of capital are always possible, changing the pressures on the value of the Hong Kong dollar. In order to maintain its fixed exchange rate the authority should neutralize these pressures on the currency's value by selling or buying US dollars and Hong Kong dollars.

  The monetary supply depends on the capital in - and outflows, and so an independent monetary policy is not possible.

- Case III: China has selected the policies of ② a fixed exchange rate (an exchange rate fluctuating within a narrow range) and ③ an independent monetary policy, and given up having ① free capital mobility.

  The Chinese authority must maintain the fixed

exchange rate and also its monetary policy independence.

If China accepted free capital mobility, the inflows and outflows of capital would cause changes in the pressures on the value of the Chinese currency, the Yuan. In order to neutralize these pressures, the Chinese authority would have to buy or sell dollars and Yuan. This would mean that the supply of the national currency was dependent on the capital flows, and that monetary policy was thus not independent.

Therefore, in order to have a fixed exchange rate and an independent monetary policy, China has to give up having free capital mobility.

5. Interest Rate Parity (IRP)

– Concept

- Concept of Parity: Parity in economics means equality in qualitative terms even if the quantitative numbers are different.

- For example, if the interest rate of a US Treasury bill of 2-year maturity is 3%, and that of a Korean government bond of 2-year maturity is 5%, then the Korean government bond pays a 2%p higher interest rate. This is the interest rate differential, $i_{Korea} - i_{USA}$.
- The aforementioned interest rate differential of 2%p is a factor causing capital inflows to Korea, since Korean deposits and Korean bonds pay higher interest rates than those of the US.
- This capital inflow increases the supply in Korea of the dollar, which should be converted to Korean Won to buy Korean assets. The dollar depreciates as a result, and the Korean Won appreciates.
- The appreciation of the Korean Won reduces the price competitiveness of Korean goods that are exported, and Korean net exports (exports − imports) decrease. This decrease in net exports leads to declines in total output and GDP, and the Korean won should finally depreciate.
- This depreciation of the Korean won offsets the benefit of the interest rate differential in the long

term. Thus, in the international financial markets, the two countries' assets have equal values in terms of quality even if their superficial interest rates are different. This is the concept of interest rate parity.

In summary, the (+) interest rate differential ($i_{Korea} - i_{USA}$) → capital inflows to Korea → increased supply of US dollars → US dollar depreciation and Korean Won appreciation → decline in Korean price competitiveness → decrease in net Korean exports → decrease in Korean GDP → Korean Won depreciation and expected exchange rate losses. The (+) interest rate differential ($i_{Korea} - i_{USA}$) and the expected loss due to the exchange rate thus cancel each other out in the long run, making the incentive for arbitrage zero if interest rate parity holds.

– Covered IRP (CIRP) and Uncovered IRP (UIRP)

- Concept of Covered IRP: In economics, the term "covered" refers to a situation in which there is no possibility of a change in value. The possibility of a change in value comes from the uncertainty of the future price. If we don't know the future price of some good, then we cannot fix its future value. But if we fix the future price of some good now, with a contract, then we can buy or sell it at this already fixed price later, irrespective of the market price.

- For example, if you make a contract to buy 1 dollar in three months at the exchange rate of 1,000 Won, you will then pay 1,000 Won in three months even if the market exchange rate has become 900 Won, or 1,100 Won.
- Here, even if you don't know the future exchange rate (900 or 1,100) you don't have to worry about it due to the contract by which you can buy 1 dollar at 1,000 Won. The concept of covered means that there is no need to worry about the uncertainty of the future price due to the already fixed price under this contract, and this contract is thus called a forward contract.
- Covered IRP (CIRP) therefore means interest rate parity between the present interest rate differential and the change in the exchange rate using the forward exchange rate. If CIRP holds, then the following equation also holds:

$$i_{Korea} - i_{USA} = \frac{F-S}{S} = \frac{E_{t+1} - E_t}{E_t}$$

where $i_{Korea} - i_{USA}$: interest rate differential,
F, E_{t+1}: forward exchange rate,
S, E_t: spot exchange rate

- Concept of Uncovered IRP (UIRP): In economics, the term "uncovered" is used in reference to a situation in which a change in value is possible. The possibility of a change in value comes from the uncertainty about the future price. If we do not fix the future price of a good now, with a contract, then we don't know how much we will have to pay to buy this good in the future. If the future price of the good rises then we will have to pay more, and if it falls we will pay less.
  - For example, if you don't make a contract to buy 1 dollar in three months at the exchange rate of 1,000 Won, then you will have to pay for it at the market exchange rate in three months.
  - Here, if the exchange rate rises in three months to a level higher than the forward exchange rate of 1,000 Won, e.g. 1,100 Won, then you will have to pay 100

Won more than the forward contract and will lose money due to the exchange rate. If the exchange rate falls to a level lower than 1,000 Won, e.g. 900 Won, then you will be able to pay 100 Won less than the forward contract and gain money due to the exchange rate. You are open to the two opposite possibilities of losing or gaining money due to the future exchange rate.

- Uncovered IRP(UIRP) thus means interest rate parity between the present interest rate differential and the expected future change in the exchange rate without a forward contract. If UIRP holds, then the following equation holds as well:

$$i_{Korea} - i_{USA} = \frac{E^a_{t+1} - E_t}{E_t}$$

where $i_{Korea} - i_{USA}$: interest rate differential,

F, E_{t+1}: forward exchange rate,

S, E_t: spot exchange rate,

E^a_{t+1}: expected future exchange rate

- Arbitrage Mechanism

■ Assumptions: Let us assume the following:

① Cost of borrowing 1 dollar in London: Libor for 3 months is at a 1.0% annual rate

② Benefit of investing in Korean Certificates of Deposit (CDs): CD for 3 months is at a 4.0% annual rate

③ Spot Won/dollar exchange rate: 1,000

④ Forward Won/dollar exchange rate (for 3 months): 1,005

■ Calculation of Arbitrage Benefit (or Incentive for Arbitrage)

- Interest rate differential: $i_{Korea} - i_{USA} = 4.0 - 1.0 = 3.0\%$

- Change of exchange rate: $S = 1{,}000$, $F = 1{,}005$

$$\frac{F-S}{S} = \frac{1{,}005 - 1{,}000}{1{,}000} = 0.005$$

However, this result shows the change for the 3-month period. And so in order to convert this to a 1-year basis we multiply it by 12/3, and to make it *a* percentage change we multiply that by 100. The aforementioned result thus becomes:

$$\frac{F-S}{S}\times\frac{12}{3}\times 100 =$$

$$\frac{1,005-1,000}{1,000}\times\frac{12}{3}\times 100 = 2.0\%$$

- Incentive for arbitrage = interest rate differential − change in exchange rate = 3.0% − 2.0% = 1.0 %p

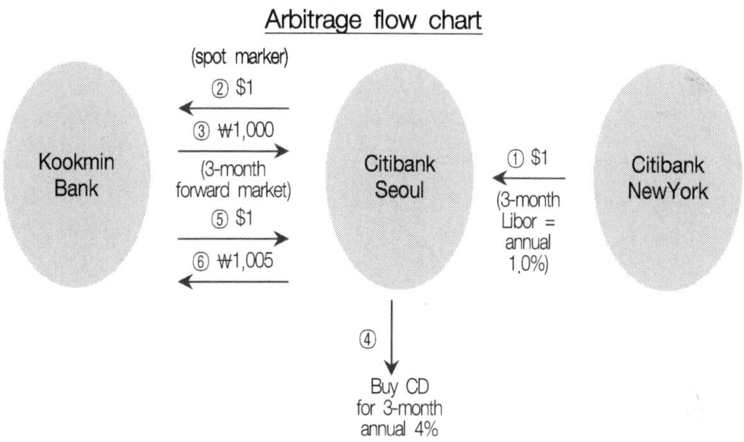

i) Interest rate differential: 4%−1%=3%p

ii) Change in exchange rate (annual, %)

$$\frac{1005-1000}{1000}\times\frac{12}{3}\times 100 = 2.0\%$$

iii) Incentive for arbitrage =3%−2%= 1%p

① Borrow $1 from Citibank N.Y.

② Sell $1 in spot market

③ Buy ₩1,000 in spot marker

④ Buy CD

⑤ Buy $1 in 3-month forward market

⑥ Sell ₩1,005 in 3-month forward market

- Does CIRP hold or not in the actual market? Why?
  - The CIRP theory means that the interest rate differential equals the change in the exchange rate in the long run, under the following assumptions: ① no constraints on international capital movements, and ② no cost of international capital movements. In this case the incentive for arbitrage converges to zero in the long run, and CIRP holds.
  - However, the actual data for Korea shows that the incentive for arbitrage has almost always been positive, i.e. that CIRP does not hold in Korea. Why not?

    First, the aforementioned assumptions are not realistic. There are actually always some constraints on and also some costs of international capital movements.

    Second, an emerging market country needs to have the dollar stay in its foreign exchange market. If the incentive for arbitrage is zero, then there is no reason for the dollar to come into the Korean market since there is no benefit.
  - From the investors' viewpoint, therefore, the positive incentive for arbitrage is a risk premium for taking

on risky currency assets, which guarantees them a positive return.

From the viewpoint of an emerging market country, Korea for example, this positive incentive for arbitrage is a cost paid to keep the dollar in the Korean market. It is however less costly and less inconvenient than borrowing dollars from the international market.

6. Effects of Depreciation Policy

- **What effects do the depreciation of a currency have on the macro economy?**

  - Exports: If all other factors remain constant, the depreciation of a country's currency boosts the price competitiveness of the country's products. The net exports of this country therefore increase.

    - But if other countries follow suit and have their currencies depreciate also, then the depreciation effect should be offset.

- Output: If the exports of a country increase then the total demand of the economy increases and its output then also expands.

- If the output of a country expands, then should its employment also increase? This is not a simple question.
  - First, the expansion in output should cause some increase in employment. But how much is the key. If the increase in output is mainly from the manufacturing sector, using capital and equipment intensively, then the increase in employment will not be considerable. This is the trend in major OECD countries recently.
  - Second, depreciation is a factor affecting inflation due to the rise in imported goods' prices. The expansion in output is also a factor causing inflation due to the increase in total demand in the economy. Therefore, after depreciation a rise in inflation is highly possible.

  Inflation reduces the real disposable income of the

people if their nominal income does not increase proportionally to the inflation. They should reduce some of their consumption expenditures, mainly in the service sector since it is impossible to cut their indispensible consumption in other sectors.

Service sector employment should decrease considerably after depreciation, but the employment in the manufacturing sector may increase slightly. Total employment in the economy as a whole may decline.

– Debate over Currency Manipulation

■ Concept of Currency Manipulation

- Currency manipulation means an intentional and artificial intervention in the foreign exchange market in order to change the value of the national currency. After the intervention, the value of the national currency deviates from its market equilibrium value.
- In theory there are two ways of manipulation – making the national currency undervalued, and making it overvalued. In reality, however, currency manipulation refers to actions to make the national currency undervalued in comparison with its equilibrium level that reflects the economy's funda-

mentals.

- Intervention to cause an appreciation of the national currency refers to actions to defend the value of the national currency against speculative attacks aimed at causing the national currency's value to fall steeply. Such defensive actions are generally accepted in the international community, and are not criticized as currency manipulation.

■ Effects of Currency Manipulation

- If a country manipulates its national currency to make it undervalued, then the products of this country become cheaper when paid for in foreign currencies (see Week 10).
- Currency manipulation improves the price competitiveness of this country's products, but in an unfair way. The trading partner countries should face worsened price competitiveness and declines in their net exports.
- This issue of unfair price competitiveness should lead to retaliatory tariffs imposed by the trading partner countries to protect their markets.

■ Criteria of Currency Manipulation

- Current Account Surplus: The current account is composed mainly of the country's net exports, i.e. its exports minus its imports. If the exports exceed the imports, then the current account runs a surplus resulting in inflows of foreign capital.

  If the inflows of foreign capital increase, then some part of this should be converted into the national currency and some other part should remain as foreign deposits. Ultimately, the increase in the supply of a foreign currency causes a decline in the relative value of that currency in this country.

  In contrast, the relative value of the national currency should rise, meaning an appreciation of the national currency.

  But if a country's currency has not appreciated significantly despite a continuous surplus in its current account, it can be argued that this country is a currency manipulator.

- Increase of Foreign Reserves: The foreign reserves are the assets in foreign currencies held by the central bank of a country. Almost all countries hold foreign reserve assets, in preparation for cases of emergency. Increases in their foreign reserves can be explained in two ways:

The first is profits from investment. If the assets are invested in bonds, or in deposits, then there should be some interest earned. The second reason for an increase in the foreign reserves is a change in the market value of the foreign reserve assets.

However, an increase in the foreign reserves due to investment should be within a certain range that is rationally understandable in view of market variables.

If a country's foreign reserves increase to an extent that is not explainable by market variables, then this country can be suspected of being a currency manipulator. It is assumed to have purchased the dollar by selling the national currency to cause the national currency to depreciate.

- Real Effective Exchange Rate Index (REERI): The REERI shows the value of the national currency. The REERI is set at 100 for a selected base year, and any increase in the REERI indicates a rise in the national currency's value.

If a country's REERI remains stable within a narrow range even despite a continuous and massive current account surplus, then it can be suspected that the REERI is being artificially managed by the foreign exchange authority.

If there had not been any currency manipulation, then the REERI would have been much higher than its present level.

(Week 12)

IS-LM Model: John Hicks and Alvin Hansen

1. The Goods Market and the IS Relationship

- **Concept: IS Relationship shows equilibrium in the Goods Market**

  ■ In a situation of equilibrium in the goods market, production (Y) must equal the demand for goods in the long run. The equilibrium condition in the goods market is thus the following:

$$Y = C(Y - T) + I(Y, i) + G \cdots\cdots \text{ IS Relationship}$$

where Y: total output of the economy,
C: consumption,
I: investment,
G: government spending,
T: government taxes,
i: the interest rate

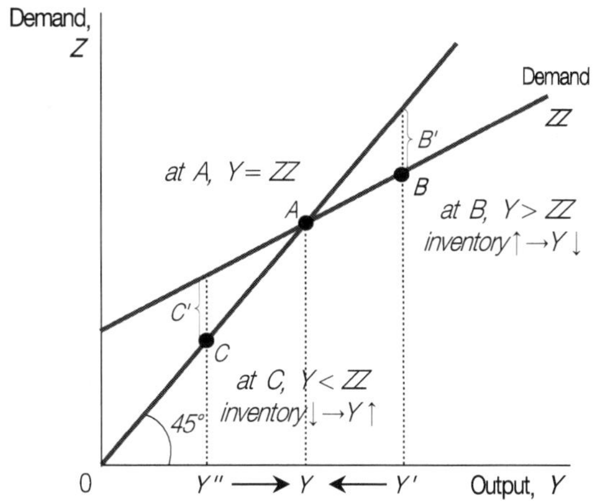

- For a given interest rate, the demand (ZZ) is an increasing function of output, and the demand curve (ZZ) shows an upward slope.
  - If output increases, then income and disposable income also increase. This increase in disposable income causes a rise in consumption. If consumption rises then the inventory declines and investment and total demand both increase:

$$Y\uparrow \rightarrow (Y-T)\uparrow \rightarrow C\uparrow \rightarrow \text{inventory}\downarrow \rightarrow I\uparrow \rightarrow \text{Demand } (ZZ)\uparrow$$

- But the slope of the demand (ZZ) is lower than that

of the output (Y). Why?

- First, if output increases then disposable income increases also, but the resulting expansion in consumption depends on the marginal propensity to consume (MPC), which is less than 1.
- Second, if output increases then investment also increases, in response to the decline in inventory caused by the increased consumption. But investment also depends on the uncertain future investment prospects.

■ At point A, the output (Y) and total demand (ZZ) intersect, showing where the economy is in equilibrium.

- At point B, the demand (ZZ) is lower than the output (Y') by B', and the inventory increases. Investment and output thus decline ($Y' \rightarrow Y$), and the economy converges to equilibrium.
- At point C, the demand (ZZ) is higher than output (Y'') by C' and inventory shrinks. Investment and output thus increase ($Y'' \rightarrow Y$), and the economy converges to equilibrium.

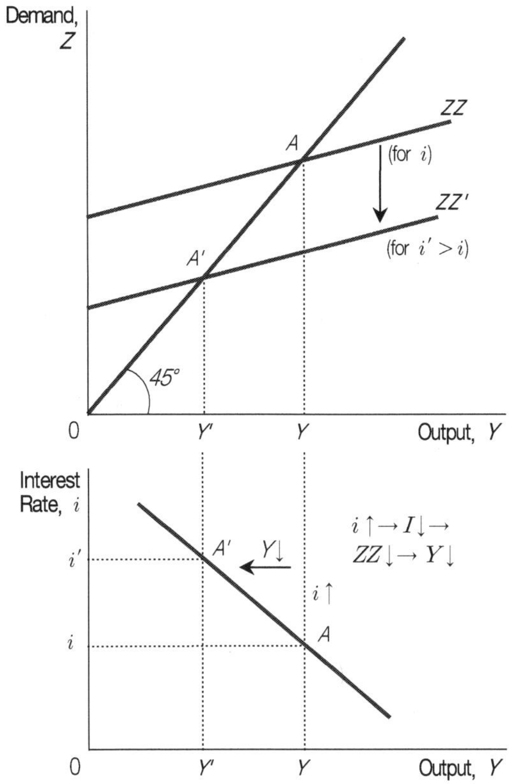

- Derivation of IS Curve

- The IS curve is a relationship between the interest rate i and output Y. It analyzes the effects of changes in the interest rate i on output Y.

- If the interest rate rises, then investment falls. This decrease in investment causes declines in demand and output:

$$i \uparrow (i - i') \rightarrow I(Y, i) \downarrow \rightarrow$$
$$ZZ \downarrow (ZZ \rightarrow ZZ') \rightarrow Y \downarrow (Y \rightarrow Y')$$

- We get the IS curve connecting two points (Y, i) and (Y', i'):

– Shift of the IS Curve

- If the government raises taxes, then the IS curve shifts to the left.
  - At a given interest rate, a rise in taxes causes a decrease in disposable income. If disposable income decreases then consumption, investment, demand and output all decline as well. The rise in taxes thus brings about decreases in output for all levels of the interest rate, and the IS curve shifts leftward:

$$T \uparrow \rightarrow (Y - T) \downarrow \rightarrow C \downarrow \rightarrow I \downarrow \rightarrow$$
$$ZZ \downarrow \rightarrow Y \downarrow \rightarrow \text{IS curve shift leftward}$$

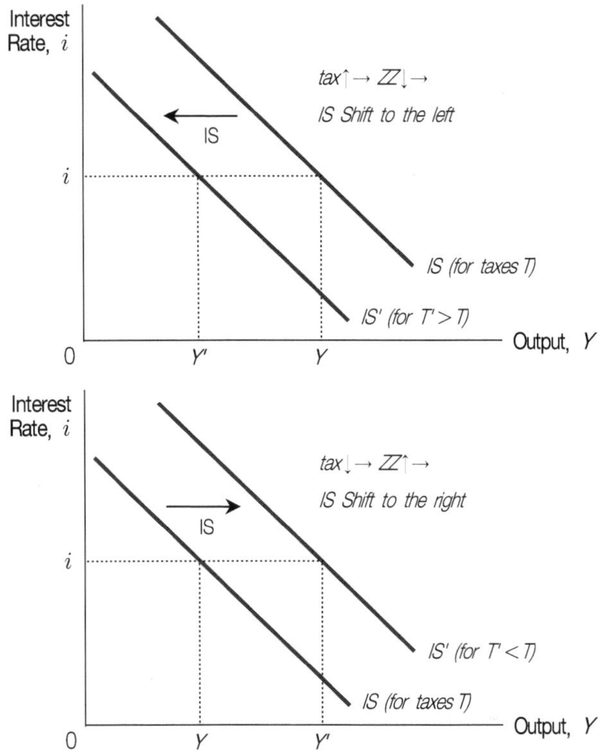

- If the government cuts taxes, the IS curve shifts to the right.
  - At a given interest rate, a reduction in taxes results in an increase in disposable income. If disposable income increases then consumption, investment, demand and output all increase as well. Thus the

decrease in taxes causes increased output at all levels of the interest rate, and the IS curve shifts to the right:

$T\downarrow \rightarrow (Y-T)\uparrow \rightarrow C\uparrow \rightarrow I\uparrow \rightarrow$
$ZZ\uparrow \rightarrow Y\uparrow \rightarrow$ IS curve shift rightward

2. Financial Markets and the LM Relationship

- **Concept: The LM Relationship shows the equilibrium in the Financial Markets:**

$(M/P) = Y \cdot L(i)$ ··················· LM Relationship

■ The real money supply (M/P) must be equal to the real money demand $\{Y \cdot L(i)\}$.

- **Derivation of LM Curve**

■ We assume that the real money supply is given by the

central bank, and so $M^s = (M/P)$ is assumed to be vertical.

- For a given Y, the real money demand is a decreasing function of the interest rate i, because under the liquidity preference theory the interest rate is an opportunity cost of holding money.

- The LM curve is a relationship between the interest rate and output, and so we analyze the effects of changes in output Y on the interest rate i.

    - If the output increases then the demand for money grows, but the supply of money is assumed to be given by the central bank, and that is vertical. The interest rate thus rises.

    There is a positive relationship between output and the interest rate (Y, i). Connecting the two equilibrium points in the financial markets, $A(Y, i)$ and $A'(Y', i')$, we see that the LM curve shows an upward slope:

$Y \uparrow (Y \rightarrow Y') \rightarrow M^d \uparrow (M^d \rightarrow M^{d'})$, but $M^s = (M/P)$ is given $\rightarrow i \uparrow (i \rightarrow i')$, LM curve slopes upward

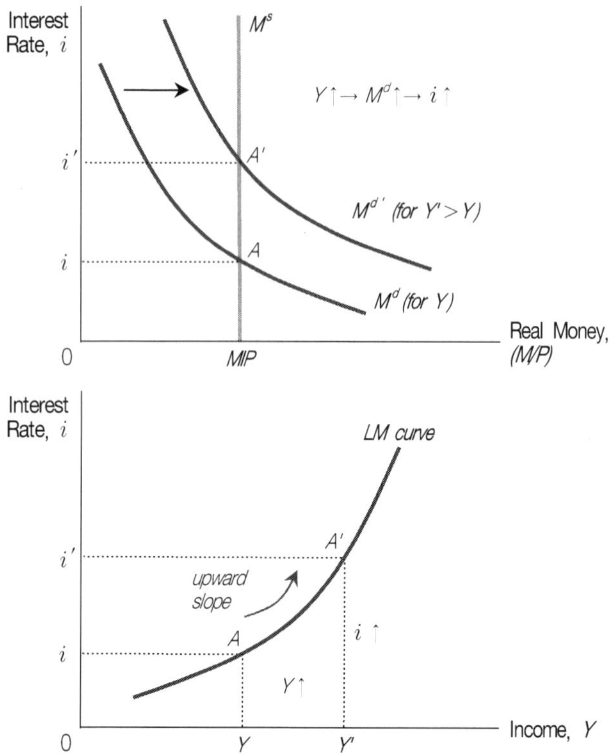

– Shift of LM Curve

- For a given Y, if the monetary supply increases, $M^s = (M/P)\uparrow$, and so the interest rate falls at any level of Y, $i\downarrow$. The LM curve thus shifts downward.

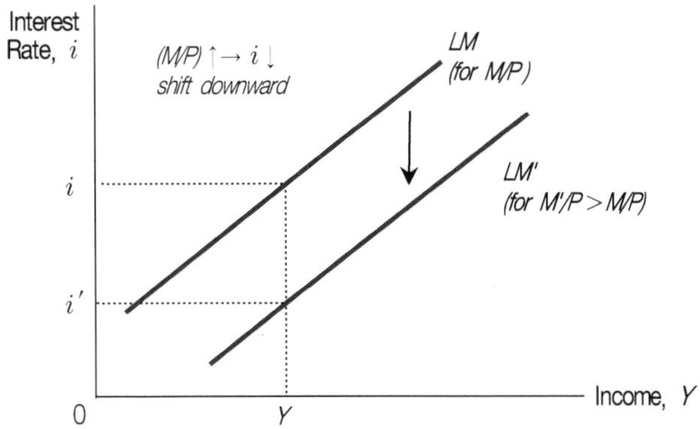

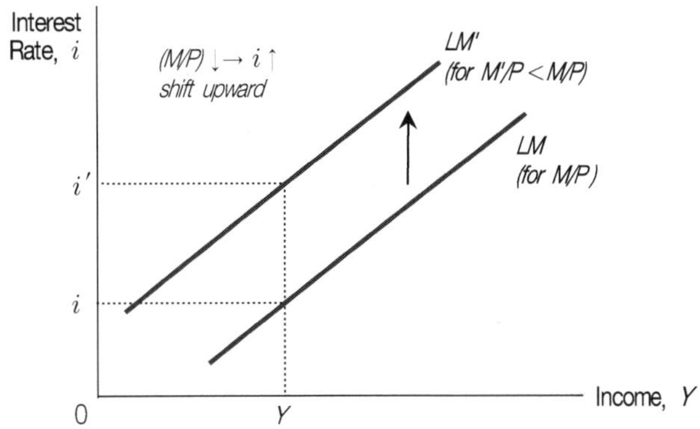

- For a given Y, if the monetary supply decreases, $M^s = (M/P)\downarrow$, and so the interest rate rises at any level of Y, $i\uparrow$. The LM curve therefore shifts upward:

3. The IS-LM Model

– Concept: Combination of IS and LM models

- IS Relationship: The IS relationship stems from the condition that the supply of goods must be equal to the demand for goods:

$$Y = C(Y - T) + I(Y, i) + G,\ i \uparrow \rightarrow Y \downarrow$$

- LM Relationship: The LM relationship stems from the condition that the supply of money must be equal to the demand for money:

$$(M/P) = Y \cdot L(i),\ Y \uparrow \rightarrow i \uparrow$$

- If we put the IS and LM relationships altogether, then the supply of goods must be equal to the demand for goods, and the supply of money must be equal to the demand for money:

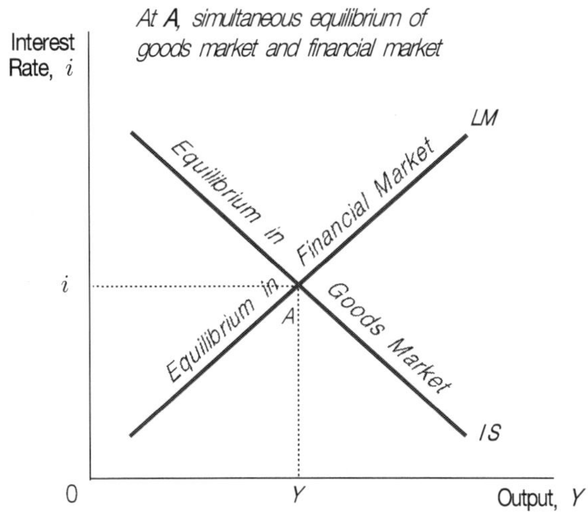

– Fiscal Policy with IS-LM Model

- Fiscal expansion

  - An increase in government expenditure causes increases in demand and output. The IS Curve thus shifts to the right:

$$G\uparrow \rightarrow \text{demand},$$

$$\{C(Y-T)+I(Y,i)+G\uparrow\}\uparrow \rightarrow Y\uparrow$$

First there is a shift of the IS curve, due to the increase in output by the multiplier effect:

$$Y = \Delta G(1 + \text{MPC} + \text{MPC}^2 + \text{MPC}^3 + + + + +)$$
$$= \Delta G / (1 - \text{MPC})$$

Second, due to the rise in the interest rate there are two offsetting effects of this ΔY:

① Crowding-out effect: If government spending increases, then the supply of government bonds expands and the interest rate rises (assuming the total credit availability remains constant).

The rising interest rate causes declines in investment and output. The IS Curve thus shifts somewhat to the left.

② Appreciation effect: If the interest rate rises due to the increase in output, then there may be some inflows of foreign capital and an appreciation of the currency.

With these two offsetting effects, the IS Curve shifts somewhat to the left:

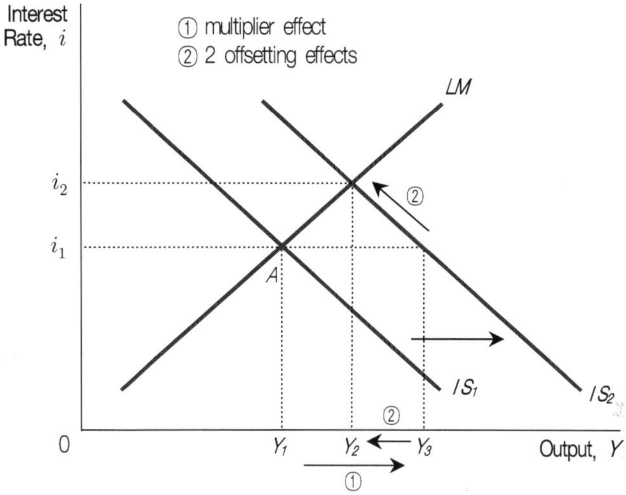

– Monetary Policy with IS-LM Model

- The IS-LM Model shows that an increase in the monetary aggregate influences income by causing lower interest rates and increased investment. This is the monetary transmission mechanism:

$$(M/P)\uparrow \{(M/P) \rightarrow (M'/P)\} \rightarrow i\downarrow (i \rightarrow i')$$
$$\rightarrow I\uparrow \rightarrow Y\uparrow (Y \rightarrow Y')$$

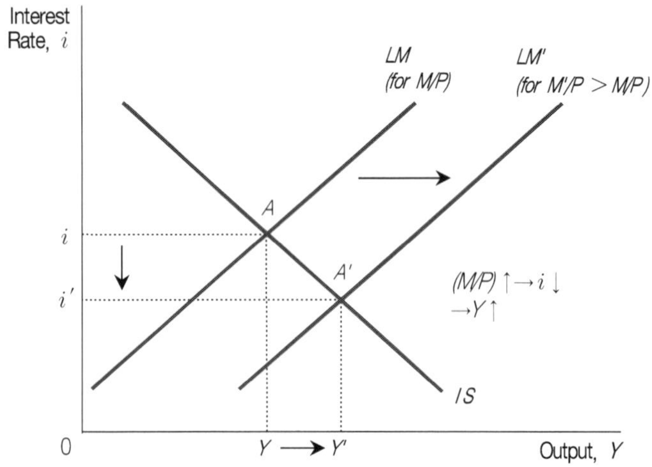

– IS-LM Model and the Liquidity Trap

- When the interest rate is extremely low, as in the situation of a so-called liquidity trap, then an expansionary fiscal policy $(G\uparrow, T\downarrow)$ is more effective than an expansionary monetary policy $\{(M/P)\uparrow\}$.

- We compare the effectiveness of expansionary fiscal policy $(G\uparrow, T\downarrow)$ with that of expansionary monetary policy $\{(M/P)\uparrow\}$, under the assumption that the economy is located in the equilibrium A.

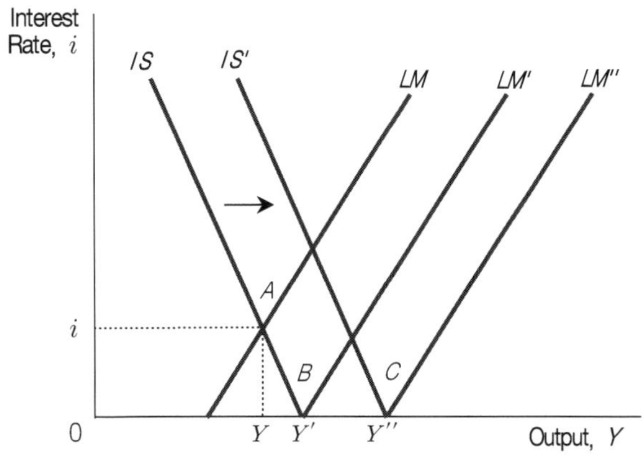

IS+LM: A(Y, i)
IS+LM': B$(Y', 0)$ $Y\uparrow (Y \rightarrow Y')$
IS+LM'': B$(Y', 0)$ no increase in Y
IS'+LM'': C$(Y'', 0)$ $Y\uparrow (Y' \rightarrow Y'')$

- An expansionary monetary policy $\{(M/P)\uparrow\}$ is effective in causing an increase in output (Y) only up to B $(Y \rightarrow Y')$.

  Beyond Y', even if the LM curve shifts further to the right due to an increase in the monetary aggregate $\{(M/P)\uparrow\}$, the intersection of the IS and LM curves is still B (if the IS curve doesn't move). Thus, the equilibrium output cannot be raised to a level higher than Y'.

- But if the IS curve shifts to the right due to expansionary fiscal policy $(G\uparrow,\ T\downarrow)$, then the intersection of the IS and LM curves moves to the right even beyond Y'. Thus an expansionary fiscal policy is more effective than an expansionary monetary policy, if the interest rate is extremely low:

- Policy Mix of IS-LM

- Let us assume that the initial equilibrium is at A, the intersection of the IS and the LM curves. If investment declines due to an external shock, then the IS curve shifts to the left($IS \rightarrow IS'$)(①).
  - If there had been no policy action, then the economy would have been at point A' with output Y'.
  - A monetary expansion can shift the LM curve to the right ($LM \rightarrow LM'$)(②).
  - A fiscal expansion can also shift the IS curve to the right ($IS' \rightarrow IS''$)(③).
  - In total, with a policy mix of monetary and fiscal expansion, the output increases from Y' to Y''.

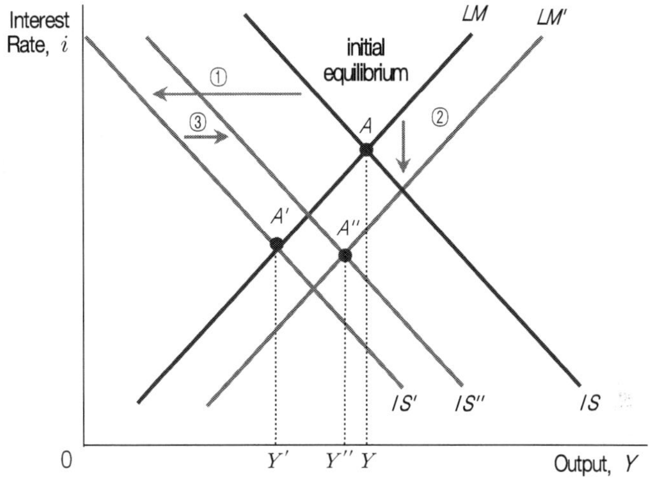

① external shock
② monetary expansion
③ fiscal expansion

(Week 13)

IS-LM and AD-AS Models

1. Aggregate Demand (AD)

– Derivation of AD Curve

■ From the IS-LM relationship, we can derive the relationship between prices (P) and output (Y):

$$LM: M/P = Y \cdot L(i),$$

$$IS: Y = C(Y-T) + I(Y, i) + G,$$

$$AD: Y = Y(M/P, G, T)$$

- If the price level rises, then the real money supply decreases and the LM curve shifts to the left raising the interest rate. The rising interest rate leads to decreases in investment, total demand and output:

$$P\uparrow (P \rightarrow P') \rightarrow \{(M/P)\uparrow)\}\downarrow \rightarrow i\uparrow$$

$$\rightarrow I\{Y(+), i(-)\uparrow\}\downarrow \rightarrow \text{demand } \{C(Y-T)+$$

$$I(Y, i\uparrow)\downarrow + G\}\downarrow \rightarrow Y\downarrow (Y \rightarrow Y')$$

We thus have the relationship that $P\uparrow \rightarrow Y\downarrow$, and the AD curve has a downward slope:

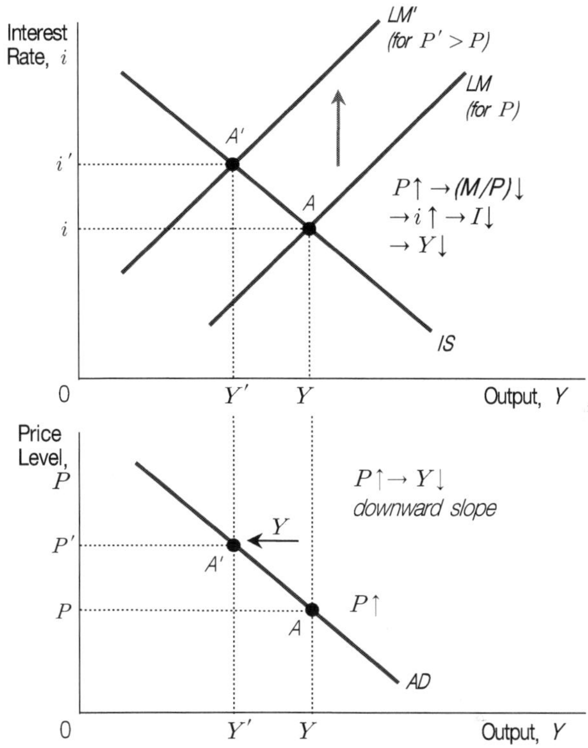

– Expansionary Monetary Policy and the AD Curve

- An expansionary monetary policy through increasing the money supply causes shifts to the right of the LM and the AD curves at a given *P*.
  - The increase in the money supply lowers the interest rate, which causes investment and output to increase:

$$(M/P)\uparrow \ \rightarrow i\downarrow (i \rightarrow i') \rightarrow I\uparrow \rightarrow \ Y\uparrow (Y \rightarrow Y')$$

- **Expansionary Fiscal Policy and the AD Curve**

■ If government spending increases, then the IS and AD curves shift to the right at a given P.

• The increase in government spending leads to increases in demand and output:

$G\uparrow \rightarrow$ demand$\{C(Y-T)+I(Y,i)+G\uparrow\}\uparrow$

$\rightarrow \ Y\uparrow (Y \rightarrow Y')$ and $i\uparrow (i \rightarrow i'')$

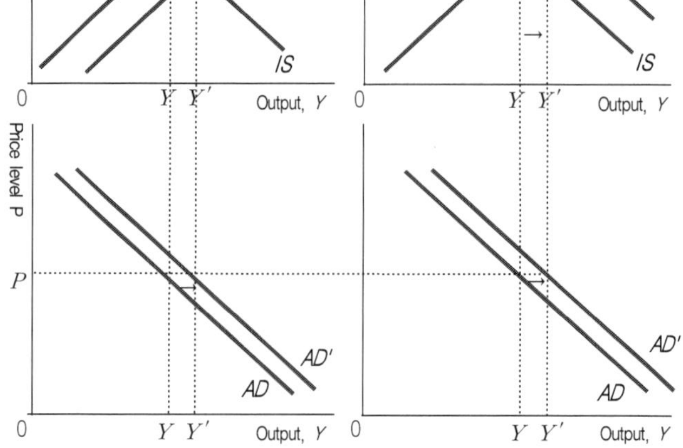

2. Aggregate Supply (AS)

– Derivation of AS Curve

■ From the labor market, we can derive the relationship between prices (P) and output (Y).

- The price level depends upon the price expectations (P^e) and the wages (W):

$$P = P^e \cdot f(W)$$

- Wages depend on the labor market situation, especially the unemployment rate (u). If the unemployment rate rises then job seekers become relatively weaker in their wage negotiations. There is thus a negative relationship between wages (W) and the unemployment rate (u).

  And if output increases, then the demand for labor grows and the unemployment rate falls. There is thus a negative relationship between the unemployment rate and output.

  Combining these two negative relationships, we have a positive relationship between wages (W) and output (Y):

$$W = f\{\overset{-}{u}(\overset{-}{Y})\} = f(\overset{+}{Y})$$

- Thus, in summary, we have the following AS relationship:

$$P = P^e \cdot f(W) = P^e \cdot f(\overset{+}{Y})$$

Because there is a positive relationship between P and Y, we see an upward sloping AS curve:

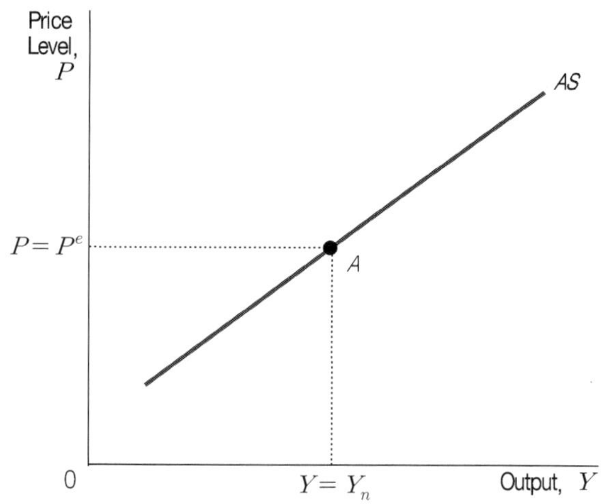

3. Equilibrium of AD-AS Model in Short Run, and in Long Run

- **Concept: We have the equilibrium output Y, from AD: $Y = Y(M/P, G, T)$ and AS: $P = P^e \cdot f(Y)$**
  - P^e determines the position of the AS curve and affects the equilibrium.
    - In the short run, P^e is given as expected by the wage setters.
    - But over time P^e changes, causing the AS curve to shift and changing the equilibrium.

- **From short-run equilibrium to long-run equilibrium**
  - Short-run equilibrium: In the short run the economy may be located at the equilibrium A (Y, P), which is higher than Y_n (the natural level of output), by the intersection of the AD and the AS curves.

  - Long-run equilibrium: Over time, however, because $P > P^e$ and $Y > Y_n$ at A, P^e rises and shifts the AS curve upward until Y decreases to return to Y_n:

$Y > Y_n$ and $P > P^e \rightarrow W\uparrow \rightarrow P\uparrow \rightarrow (M/P\uparrow)\downarrow \rightarrow i\uparrow \rightarrow Y\downarrow (Y \rightarrow Y_n) \rightarrow$ AS curve shift leftward

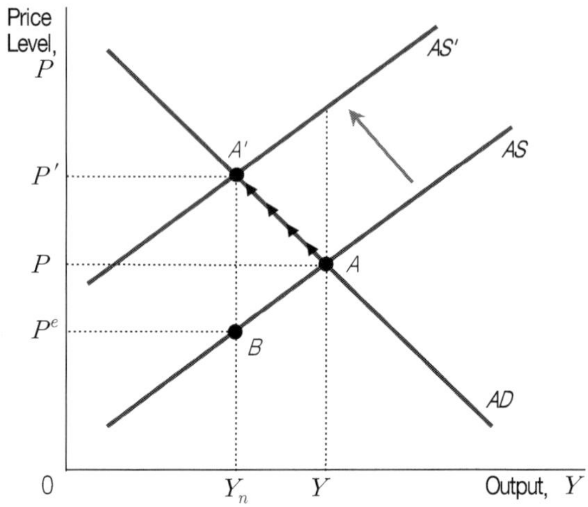

$A\ (Y, P)$: Initial equilibrium in the short run, but $Y > Y_n$, $P > P^e$

$A'\ (Y_n, P')$: Long-run equilibrium after shift of AS curve to the left $(AS \rightarrow AS')$

4. Effects of Monetary Expansion (MP)

– **Assumptions**

■ The economy is located at the natural level of output (Y_n).

■ The intersection of the AD and AS curves is at $A(Y_n, P=P^e)$.

■ The intersection of the IS and LM curves is at $A(Y_n, i)$.

– **Short-run effect of monetary expansion**

■ A monetary expansion causes the AD curve to shift to the right:

$$(M\uparrow /P) \rightarrow \overrightarrow{AD}: Y=Y(\overrightarrow{M\uparrow /P}, G, T) \text{ and}$$
$$AD \rightarrow AD'$$

• The intersection of the AD' and AS curves is at $A'(Y', P')$.

■ A monetary expansion causes the LM curve to shift to the right also:

$(M\uparrow /P) \rightarrow \overrightarrow{LM}$: $(\overrightarrow{M\uparrow /P}) = Y \cdot L(i)$ and $LM \rightarrow LM'$

- The intersection of the IS and LM curves is at $A'(Y', i')$.

■ In the short run, the expansionary monetary policy causes the interest rate to fall and output to rise.

Short run: $(M\uparrow /P) \rightarrow i\downarrow (i \rightarrow i') \rightarrow Y\uparrow (Y_n \rightarrow Y')$

- **Medium - and long-run effects of monetary expansion**

■ At $A'(Y', P')$ in the AD−AS model, $Y' > Y_n$ and $P' > P = P^e$, so $P^e\uparrow$ and the AS curve shifts upward to reach the natural output level at A"(Y_n, P'')".

■ At $A'(Y', P')$ in the IS-LM model, $Y' > Y_n$ so $P\uparrow \rightarrow (M/P\uparrow)\downarrow \rightarrow i\uparrow$ and the LM curve shifts backward cancelling the effect of the LM shift to the right by $(M\uparrow /P)\uparrow$.

■ In the long run, the short-run effect of monetary expansion is offset by the effect of the rising price level ($P' \rightarrow P''$) and the rising interest rate ($i' \rightarrow i$), and output finally returns to its original level (Y_n).

Long run: Money is neutral

Short-run effect (①)

$(M\uparrow / P) \rightarrow$

AD shift rightward

LM shift downward

$A(Y_n, P^e) \rightarrow A'(Y', P')$

$A'(Y', i')$

Long-run effect (②)

at A', $P' > P^e$, $Y' > Y_n$

AS shift upward

LM shift backward

by rising $i(i' \rightarrow i)$

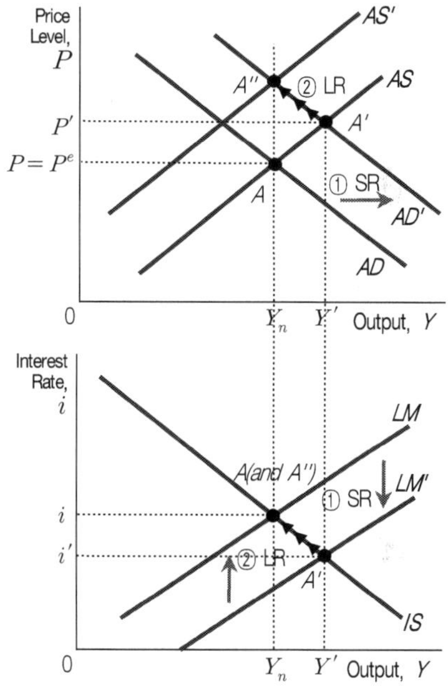

---

5. Decrease in Budget Deficit (Fiscal Contraction)

- **Assumptions**

  - The economy is located at the natural output level (Y_n).

  - The intersection of the AD and AS curves is at $A(Y_n, P=P^e)$.

  - The intersection of the IS and LM curves is at $A(Y_n, i)$.

- **Short-run effect of fiscal contraction**

  - Fiscal contraction shifts the AD curve to the left:

$$G\downarrow \rightarrow \overleftarrow{AD}: Y = Y(M/\overleftarrow{P, G}\downarrow, T) \text{ and}$$

$$AD \rightarrow AD'$$

    - The intersection of the AD' and AS curves is at $A'(Y', P')$.

  - Fiscal contraction shifts the IS curve to the left as well:

$G\downarrow \rightarrow \overleftarrow{IS}: Y = C(Y-T) + I(Y,i) + G\downarrow$ and $IS \rightarrow IS'$

- The intersection of the IS' and LM' curves is at $A'(Y', i')$.

■ In the short run, a fiscal contraction causes the interest rate to fall and output to decrease:

Short run: $G\downarrow \rightarrow i\downarrow (i \rightarrow i')$ and $Y\downarrow (Y_n \rightarrow Y')$

- **Medium - and long-run effects of fiscal contraction**

■ At $A'(Y', P')$ in the AD−AS model, $Y' < Y_n$ and $P' < P = P^e$, so $P^e\downarrow$ and the AS curve shifts downward to reach the natural level of output at $A''(Y_n)$.

■ At $A'(Y', P')$ in the IS-LM model, $Y' < Y_n$ so $P\downarrow \rightarrow (M/P\downarrow)\uparrow \rightarrow i\downarrow (i' \rightarrow i'')$ and the LM curve shifts to the right to reach the natural output level at $A''(Y_n)$:

Short-run effect(①)

$G\downarrow \rightarrow$

AD shift leftward

IS shift leftward

$A(Y_n, P=P^e) \rightarrow A'(Y', P')$

$A(Y_n, i) \rightarrow A'(Y', i')$

Long-run effect(②)

at A', $P' < P^e$, $Y' < Y_n$

AS shift rightward

LM shift rightward

$A'(Y', P') \rightarrow A''(Y_n, P'')$

$A'(Y', i') \rightarrow A''(Y_n, i'')$

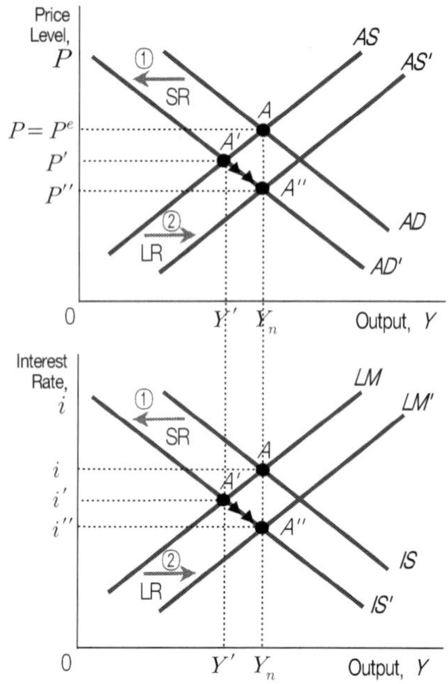

(Week 14)

IS-LM Model: An Extension to the Open Economy

1. Equilibrium in Goods Market

– Extension to NX, and IRP

- We can extend the IS model including net exports and IRP (interest rate parity).

  - Imports depend positively on the national output and positively also on the exchange rate.

    If the national output increases then the national income rises, causing an increase in imports. If the national currency appreciates, then the prices of imported goods fall and imports increase.

  - Exports depend positively on the foreign output and negatively on the exchange rate.

    If the foreign output increases then foreign income rises, causing greater demand for the national product, exports. If the national currency appreciates then the prices of the nation's goods in foreign countries rise and exports decline.

  - Interest rate differential $i-i^*$: if the national interest rate rises, then there are negative effects on out put:

    ① The rising interest rate causes the cost of investment to increase and so investment declines, causing decreases in total demand and output.

② The rising interest rate results in a wider interest rate differential, and higher returns on national bonds. Capital inflows thus increase, causing the national currency to appreciate which leads to declines in exports, total demand and output.

■ Reflecting the aforementioned factors, the IS model can be shown as follows:

$$IS: Y = C(Y-T) + I(Y, i) + G + X(Y^{*}, E) - M(Y, E)$$

where E: exchange rate,
↑ appreciation, ↓ depreciation

$$IS: Y = C(Y-T) + I(Y, i) + G + NX(Y, Y^{*}, E)$$

$$IS: Y = C(Y-T) + I(Y, i) + G + NX[Y, Y^{*}, i - i^{*}, E]$$

* Here, if interest rate parity holds then this interest rate differential should be offset by the expected depreciation of the national currency in the long run. But in reality, as we have already seen in Week 11, interest rate parity does not hold. We thus put the interest rate differential and the

exchange rate altogether as the factors affecting NX.

2. Equilibrium in the Financial Markets

- **Even in an open economy, the real money supply must equal the demand for money.**

  - If the supply of real money increases, then the interest rate falls.

  - If the demand for money increases due to an expansion in output, then the interest rate rises:

$$LM: M/P = Y \cdot L(i)$$

$$(M^s = M/P) \uparrow \rightarrow i \downarrow,$$

$$Y \uparrow \rightarrow \{M^d = Y \cdot L(i)\} \uparrow \rightarrow i \uparrow$$

3. Effects of Policy in an Open Economy

- **IS-LM with IRP not holding**

$$IS: Y = C(Y-T) + I(Y, i) + G$$

$$+NX[Y, Y^*, i-i^*, E]$$

$$LM: M/P = Y \cdot L(i)$$

– Effects of Fiscal Policy in an Open Economy

$$IS: Y = C(Y-T) + I(Y, i) + G$$

$$+NX[Y, Y^*, i-i^*, E]$$

$$LM: M/P = Y \cdot L(i)$$

- Assumptions: The government increases spending from a balanced budget and without raising taxes. The government thus faces a budget deficit.

- Effects of fiscal expansion
  - The increase in government spending by ΔG leads to an increase in output $(Y \rightarrow Y'')$ at a given interest rate by the multiplier effect, causing the IS curve to shift to the right $(IS \rightarrow IS')$(see Week 1):

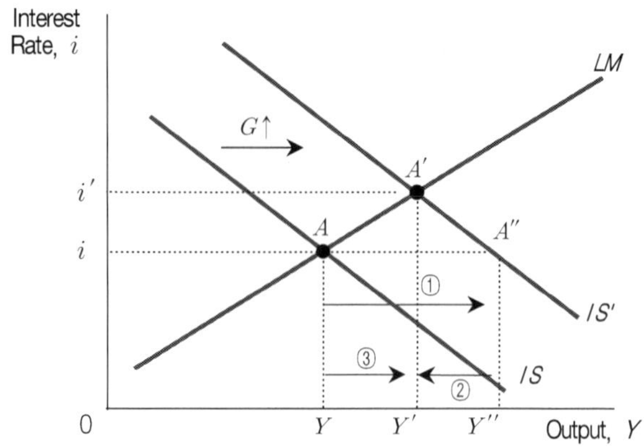

① multiplier effect of $\Delta G\uparrow$

② 2 offsetting effects of rising i

③ final effect of $\Delta G\uparrow$

- But there are two offsetting effects ($Y''\rightarrow Y'$) of the rising interest rate: the crowding-out effect and the appreciation effect (see Week 1). The output thus increases only from Y to Y':

$$\Delta G\uparrow \;\rightarrow\; Y\uparrow \;\rightarrow\; \{M^d = Y\cdot L(i)\}\uparrow$$

$$\rightarrow\; i\uparrow \;\rightarrow\; \text{crowding out and appreciation}$$

– Effects of Monetary Policy in an Open Economy

$$IS:\; Y = C(Y-T) + I(Y, i) + G + NX[Y, Y^*, i-i^*, E]$$

$$LM:\; M/P = Y\cdot L(i)$$

- If the central bank reduces the supply of money by ΔM, then the interest rate rises and the LM curve shifts to the left. We thus have the following effects :
  - The rising interest rate causes investment and output to decline.
  - The rising interest rate causes NX and output to decrease as well, through the appreciation of the national currency:

$$\{M^s = M/P\}\downarrow \rightarrow i\uparrow \rightarrow \{\text{appreciation} \rightarrow NX\downarrow,\ I(Y, i\uparrow)\downarrow\} \rightarrow Y\downarrow$$

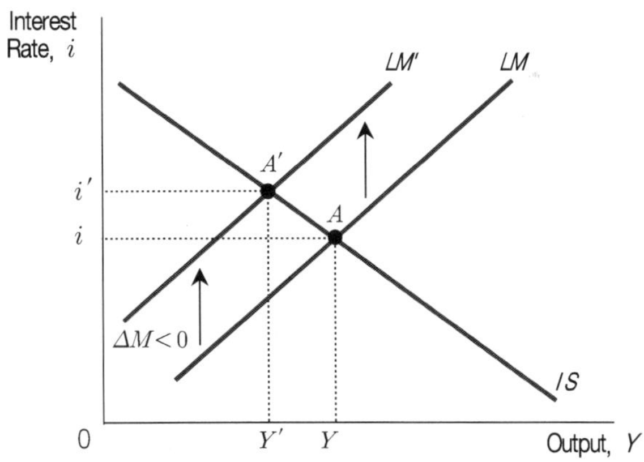

A: Intial equilibrium

A': Equilibrium after $(M/P)\downarrow \rightarrow i\uparrow (i \rightarrow i')$ $\rightarrow NX\downarrow,\ I\downarrow \rightarrow Y\downarrow (Y \rightarrow Y')$

– Fiscal Policy under Fixed and Flexible Exchange Rate Regimes

- A fiscal expansion through ΔG causes the IS curve to shift to the right.
  - Under a flexible exchange rate regime, the central bank can accept a rise in the interest rate and appreciation of the national currency, while keeping the monetary supply constant. Output thus increases from Y to Y'.
  - Under a fixed exchange rate regime, the central bank cannot accept a rise in interest rates or appreciation of the national currency. It will have to increase the supply of money to avoid these two things. The central bank gives up monetary policy as a policy instrument, but output increases more than in the case of a flexible exchange rate regime, from Y to Y'':

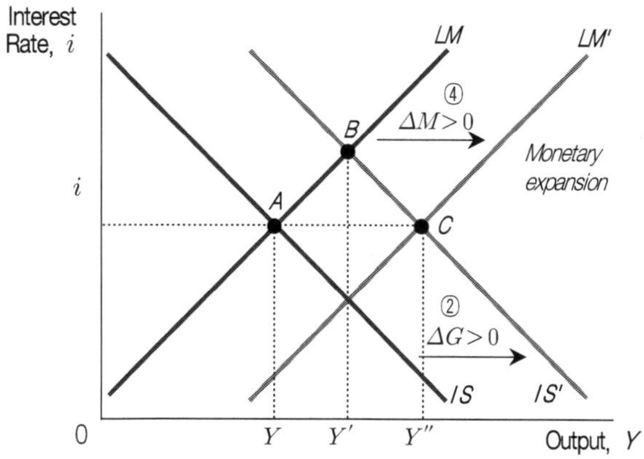

① A : Intial equilibrium

② $\Delta G\uparrow$: IS shift rightward ($IS\rightarrow IS'$)

③ B: New equilibrium under flexible exchange rato regime, without $\Delta M\uparrow\rightarrow Y\uparrow$ ($Y\rightarrow Y'$)

④ C: New equilibrium under fixed exchange rato regime, with $\Delta M\uparrow\rightarrow LM$ shift rightward ($LM\rightarrow LM'$) $Y\uparrow$ ($Y\rightarrow Y''$)

Index

(D)

(E)

(F)

(G)

(H)

(I)

(J)

(K)

(L)

(M)

(N)

(O)

(P)

(Q)

(R)

(S)

(T)

(U)

(V)

(W)

(Y)